1967

This Is It!

Lowell Tarling

Artwork by Martin Sharp

ETT IMPRINT
Exile Bay

ETT Imprint

PO Box R1906, Royal Exchange NSW Australia

Document creation: Linda Ruth Brooks Publishing
www.lindaruthbrooks.com

First published by Generation Books in 1990

This edition published by ETT Imprint, Exile Bay 2020

Cover design: © Joel Tarling 2013

Artwork © Martin Sharp

ISBN: 978-1-922384-13-3 (eBook)
ISBN: 978-1-922384-12-6 (paper)

Author website
www.lowelltarling.com.au

A novel

Table of Contents

Thanks

Martin Sharp for encouragement and permission to reproduce his artwork.

Musical assistance from Robert Wolfgramm, Jason Whalley and*Spectres of André* – a bandcomprising David Jensen, Hamish Mitchie, Alex Mitchie and Derek Barg.

And especially Robbie, Amber, Joel and Zoë – my family – for putting up with my late nights and for listening to me read sections of the book over and over and over. Thanks for your comments, suggestions and patience.

Acknowledgements

Some of Martin Sharp's pictures have previously appeared in Oz Magazine, *Martin Sharp Cartoons* (Scripts Pty Ltd), *People, Politics and Pop* by Craig McGregor (Ure Smith), *Pop* by Peter Draffin (Scripts Pty Ltd) and the *Sydney Morning Herald.* Other drawings have never before appeared in print.

Kevin Broadhurst, founder of the Linda Lee record label for granting permission for the use of the name and design of his label.

Editorial assistance and comments from Allan Broadhurst, Merryn Cosgrove, Peter Draffin, Neale Farnell, Martin Fowler, Neil Graham, Bob Harris, Liz Hughes, David Jensen, Karl Jensen, Peter Jensen, Joe McGuinness, Perry Mason, Adrian Rawlins, Clayton Simms, Tony Stacey, Glen Tetley, Eldean Ward, Greg Weight and Robert Wolfgramm.

Musical assistance also includes Brett Copeman, Nick Lyon, Mitch Hart and Paul Bryant.

Appropriations (or rip-offs – depending on how you see it) extracted from Alan Burgess, Charles Dickens, Peter Draffin, Bob Dylan, TS Eliot, Allen Ginsberg, Terry Johnson, Jack Kerouac, George Bernard Shaw and PF Sloan.

Communist Girls is written by Lowell Tarling and Robert Wolfgramm.

Lyrics to *This Is It!* written by David Jensen and Robert Wolfgramm. Music by Robert Wolfgramm.

The poem *Positively Mockerism* by Allan Broadhurst.

Extract from *White Holden Panel Van* appropriated from Adrian Roy.

Genuine letters from Vietnam by Ken Walker.

Letter from Vincent by Vincent van Gogh.

Linda Lee record label, artwork by Clayton Simms.

Generation books logo and cover design, Joel; Tarling.

Cover and interior formatting by Linda Brooks of Linda Brooks Publishing.

stormy nonsense

yesterday i closed my eyes on the passing face
of envenomed passion
which i dreamed until i lifted into the sky
& i saw stormy nonsense
& approaching faces

i dreamed of my favourite resentment
an uxorious love
which burns
& burns
through the inquietude of your soul into
the explosive pigment of heart matter.
i dreamed of black abyss
myself no more than a spinning prism
spinning myself sick
until i slid through a state of reticence
& enclosed myself in an empty tennis court
in one hand a broken armless doll
a courtful of argentinian ants
& french letters everywhere

i sat there
& watched those objects form
& deform
then tangle into mass
& gradually
like a great tongue licking into all corners of
existence, it engulfed all there was

but it would not engulf me

“Hope I die before I get old”

Pete Townsend, The Who

1

Season of the Witch

It is the best of times. It is the worst of times. It is the age of wisdom. It is the age of foolishness. It is the age of The Who and the Beatles. It is the time of Dylan. It is the season of Light. It is the season of Darkness.

Nobody is who they think they are. Everyone is whoever they want to be. It is the autumn of despair, the winter of discontent, the spring of hope. And the Summer of Love.

We have everything before us. Everything is original. Everything borrowed.

People come only in two types: those who ARE Rock and Roll and those who ain't.

*

'Why don't you actually *do* something creative!' exclaims the only interesting adult in my suburb. 'Like my brother Richard who's with London OZ magazine right now…look what he sent!'

She hands me an autographed copy of the newest Stones album, unreleased in Australia for another three months.

Autographed!

The gods have actually touched this cardboard and the Postmaster General has delivered it to her door, never knowing the extreme importance of that postie's mission.

'You can be anything you want to be.' That's her message to me and my friends.

The sister of the Great Richard of London, gives me pointers on being hip (something she can never be herself no matter what cos she's 36 years old).

*

It is 1967. I am in 6th form.

I am almost 18 and suddenly born again.

Born into the best of times.

Born into the age of wisdom.

Born into the season of the witch.

Born into the season of light.

Born into the void.

Born into the enlightenment.

Religion: we want it. Not the religion of the suburbs and the deadheads. We are the dharma bums. The new lunatics. Believers in the religion of Dylan, the Gita, the Tibetan Book of the Dead, the Dalai Lama, the Gautama Buddha and the religion of Siddhartha. Gimme some truth and gimme some neck.

Politics yep, we want it. Nude and stoned politics. The President of the United States Lyndon B Cowboy and his rival, that ugly face of Russia. Imagine them sitting together naked, tripping and making decisions. Could it be worse? No, it'd be better and you better believe it.

Tell me different and you're showing your age. *Peace and love man*, you can't imagine any president getting those words out. They don't think that way. Yes we want politics. I'm a believer. Never tell me I'm not. Never tell me I don't want nuthin. I want a lot.

I want to play guitar with my teeth. Smash a Rickenbacker. Grow long hair. I want to worship the King believing no king but the Lizard King.

I am - you are - the most important people in the world. I am famous for a minute. Gimme that minute now.

Hey reader? Are you a wrinkly-eyed, poxy-faced, short-haired, conservative, money-minded, boring old fart. If you are, put down my story. Put it down if your hair is greying. If you vote for anybody at all, stuff off. If you're old enough to be dead, go away.

Eighteen is all that counts.

How old did you say?

18.

Then you are just like me. You are the most important people too. Claim your minute. Claim it now. Tomorrow you may be dead.

We hold the key: one our parents, teachers and politicians have never heard of - Love.

Make love.

I wish I had.

Love everyone, who isn't a parent.

Love everyone, who isn't a skoolteacher.

Love everyone, who isn't a cop.

Love everyone, who isn't in government.

Love everyone, who doesn't fight in Vietnam.

Love everyone.

My name is Tom.

With no plan, no money and no direction, you and me have decided we're gonna change the world.

Anyone who isn't Rock N Roll is old. And old is the worst thing in life you can be.

You and me will be 18 forever.

AS
I WANDER
THROUGH THE BRILLIANT
STARS, I REMEMBER THROUGH THE
MISTS OF TIME
TALL IRON GATES WHICH HELD ME CAPTIVE FROM THE LIGHT OF TRUTH
LONG AGO
PRIVATE SCHOOLS
DEAR OLD BOY,
YOUR OLD SCHOOL, WHICH TAUGHT YOU TO SEEM TO BE RATHER THAN TO BE, TO PLAY RUGBY AND TO MARCH IN STEP, WHICH TAUGHT YOU TO BE A HYPOCRITE WITH DIGNITY, (AND SKILL), WHICH DELIVERED YOU FROM ITS IRON GATES WITH A REMARKABLE CERTIFICATE, ENABLING YOU TO ENTER THE WORLD OF MEN AND CONTINUE IN THE PROFITABLE PURSUITS OF THE ABOVE MENTIONED VIRTUES, IN AN ELEVATED SOCIAL STATUS, IS COLLECTING DONATIONS FOR A BUILDING FUND FOR YET ANOTHER WAR MEMORIAL
TAX DEDUCTABLE
KEEP THE BALL ROLLING
NOSTALGIC APPEAL LETTER

2

Set the Controls for the Heart of the Sun

Okay, let's get serious. This is where the skool year begins - February 1967, the start of my final year. We've just come back from holidays and my best trick was to see the *Big Show 1967* at the Sydney Stadium nearly a fortnight ago. The acts were Jeff St John & the Id, Johnny Young, the Walker Brothers, the Yardbirds (with Jimmy Page & Jeff Beck) and top of the bill - Roy Orbison.

I did other things too. I read *Huck Finn,* a 6th form text. I also bought the denim jacket I've been eyeing off and I learned the chords to Dylan's *It Takes a Lot to Laugh, it Takes a Train to Cry.* Girl-wise, I started making a play for a truly beautiful PLC girl called Stephanie whose father said it was okay for me to see her so long as I didn't date her. He said I wasn't their 'type'.

Right now it's a free period and we're waiting for Mr Devlin to teach us Vocational Guidance, a non-examinable subject. We sit around. Classmates tell me what they did over the hols and I tell em about Jimmy Page.

Jenny went to Noumea, Adrian went to Excitement City Adelaide and Ian studied the whole time except for when he picked up three days work. After that it's all about L-plates and P-plates which doesn't interest me - but it's a whole lot better than talking about who's gonna be picked as prefects.

Everyone says yeah to Ian, yeah to Jenny, yeah to Adrian - cos he's the big sports hero, yeah to this one, yeah to that one, but no to me, no to Mark and no to John Pye. Ian, Arnold, Daks, Jenny, Sue, Janet, Colin and Peter are rapt about their 100% chances of becoming prefects and wondering why me & Mark don't give a shit.

What does bother me though is that I can't see why John Pye shouldn't be in with the others, just because Peter & Daks think they're 'better' than John. I just don't git it.

I know exactly where this conversation is headed. We're now coming up to the big question – who's gonna be SKOOL CAPTAIN.

Is it I Lord?

O god this is boring. I wrote a poem called 'Adum' over the holidays, I tell them about it, just to be annoying. It goes like this: *I am an injection, a handful of sperm cells...'* but no one cares about a handful of sperm cells.

Not with the important question of who will be SKOOL CAPTAIN?

'Not John Pye.' Ha ha ha goes Peter, 'Imagine John as school captain. That's as funny as Tom or Mark with their long hair!' Ha ha har.

This is all because of my dickhead suburb, Turramurra, where parents all want their kids to be doctors, lawyers and solicitors.

It might very clever talking about poets and artists at skool. And it's real cultured to talk about Art at cocktail parties so long as nobody's kids ever wants to BE a poet, artist or muso.Who'd want an Easybeat for a son? Not my old man, that's fer sure.

I'm getting sick of all this let's-all-be-prefects talk, so I jump up on the teacher's desk and yell 'shurrup everyone!'

'Typical Tom...', sneers Arnold, '...always got to attract attention to himself' - which is what he always says, especially when I stand on tables or play my guitar on the train.

'Listen!' (here comes my Big Idea) 'If I can't *BE* a prefect, I'll *make* a prefect!'

'How?' says Greg who has never had and never will have *Imagination*.

'Same as Mr Sheen, Louie the Fly and Marlborough Country - I'll run the best advertising campaign this joint has ever seen. I'll make a slogan MEET PYE or even MEAT PYE, and I'll chalk 'Vote Pye' everywhere, from the station to the classroom. Pye is about to become famous!'

'MEAT PYE...yer crazy!'

'Catchy huh? John, if you agree, let's show em!'

'Don't rock the boat Tom, I'm certain to be School Captain', says Adrian, 'I don't want to deal with insincere votes.'

'I want to be School Captain too...' says Peter.

'And me...' says Colin.

'Me too,' says Ian.

'Well I just might put a Spaniard in the works...', and I leave it at that.

In walks Paul Gaschner, 'What goin on?'

'Oh Tom here wants to...'

'...change the world.'

'Never mind all that. I've got to tell Tom not to attend any more classes til he gets a haircut.'

'Who sez?"

'The Boss' (ie. the headmaster).

'Don't let on you've told me yet. Yer not a prefect yet. Mightn't even be one now John Pye is the new force. Anyway, here comes Devlin...' I peek out the window, 'his fly's undone'.

'How do you know?' says bright boy Daks.

'How do I KNOW??'

*

‘Good morning 6th form,’ says Mr Devlin, a young macho teacher who gave up motorbikes to become a teacher once he figured that teachers get to beat the crap out of more people than bikers.

Big chorus: ‘GOOD MORNING SUH’.

‘Be seated. I’m here to talk about Vocational Guidance…’

Yeah great. Half of us don’t know what the hell we wanna be when we leave, the others all wanna be doctors…

…cept me, who wants to be a Rock muso. And whenever I tell em that everyone looks at me like I’m nuts. In my case, the correct answer could be MALE NURSE. Yessir that’s what they reckon I was born to be.

Teachers would think I had heaps of sense if I chucked my guitar and dedicated my life to sticking needles in people, arse-wiping and emptying their potties. Yessir, a male nurse is my Destiny. Gimme that handshake.

That’s how class begins and Devlin (who’s got greaseback hair – yuk) tells the girls that the best they can hope for is Nursing. The others could ‘strive’ for a secretarial position. Except for Sue, cos she’s got brains. She could become a teacher.

Sue says she plans to be a doctor. He goes, ‘Ha ha ha, very funny my girl. A 6-year course that you’re gonna quit halfway through when you get married, fall pregnant and stay home. Now teaching…’.

Ahhh, teaching! That a good one cos she can do a 3-year diploma, get married, put in a couple of deposit-on-the-house money-earning years, get pregnant, get locked away in the suburbs for about 20 years, and when the kids have left home she’ll always have teaching ‘to fall back on’.

‘No,’ says Sue. ‘I don’t want to get married. I want to become a doctor’.

Argue, argue, argue – but Devlin won’t have it her way. Meanwhile he sticks his finger up his nose, pulls out a big bit and wipes it on a tissue, as if we hadn’t noticed. Then, cos Sue won’t shut up, Devlin gets snappy. So it’s settled. Within five years Sue will be married and pregnant. Next point.

‘This is the Information Age’, he says, picking his nose again. ‘Only the very best amongst you boys will find employment. The others? You’ll wind up DOING NOTHING. NUTHIN. Ah ha! There’s a fate for you. All those wasted years at school…’

I was thinking the same thing. All those goddam wasted years at skool when I might’ve stayed home doing something useful like growing my hair.

I see it now - talking to someone, writing, sketching, watching telly, listening to music, reading a poem, building a yurt, seeing Jimmy Page at the Sydney Stadium, dancing, laughing, being with friends, kissing, even thinking, is all nothing to him.

This stupid arsehole (who wants me to be a male nurse) reckons that if I was a skool teacher like him or a clerk in the Public Service ahhh, then I’d EXIST. And he’s grinning while telling us all this shit, dammit.

'By 1980, the Age of Robots...' he's getting all excited now because he's gonna talk about violence, '...there'll be fighting in the streets as people beg for employment. The Computer Age will be upon us and millions will be out of work. Only the top 25 per cent will have decent jobs, the ones who have proven themselves. Listen to this for comparison...' he pulls out some notes.

'School life in Hong Kong is very different to Australia's. Going to and from school in Sydney it is usual to travel on a train or bus – say – for half an hour, whereas in Hong Kong one would normally travel for say, 10 minutes.'

Why am I hearing this?

'One would never hear of a pupil not doing homework in Hong Kong, but it is a big problem here in Australia...ha ha ha,' says Mr Devlin, glancing at Mark and fiddling with his green tie. (Why do teachers always wear green and brown. I hate green and brown.)

'Sport is neglected in Hong Kong and all efforts are put into studying proper subjects. Maybe this is the reason...' big joke coming up next, I can tell, 'maybe this is the reason...'. O god, he's laughing at it himself and having three shots at it. 'Maybe this is the reason why so many Chinese wear thick glasses!'

'Do they?' questions Daks.

'Sir, sir!' says Mark, who's in my band, 'will they ever put a man on the moon?' It's a set-up question, he just wants to hear the stupid answer again.

'Who? The Chinese?'

'No', Mark replies, '...anybody?'

'Of course not, God would never allow it. It says so in the Bible.'

'Where?' asks Sue. She's nailed him.

'Where? I don't know exactly *where*,' (of course he doesn't). 'You should know these things yourself Sue. Don't you read your Bible? Anyway, back to the subject. In Hong Kong, they spend seven years in high school. Seven. Whereas in Australia we only spend six'.

'I knew that', says Mark.

'You knew they spend seven?'

'No...that we only spend six.' I crack up. So does Pye.

'What's so funny John?' says the teacher.

'Chinese glasses, sir.'

'Oh yes, ha ha ha. Plenty more jokes like that. How about some Interesting Future Facts. Did you know that according to the latest research, in 1990 only 28% of people will have jobs?'

'You said 25 per cent!' says Daks.

'That was 1980,' Devlin snaps – flustered. 'And those people will be enormously rich…'.

'Which people?"

'The people with jobs.'

'Oh.'

'It'll be a clear-cut case of the Haves and the Have-Nots. I'm sure nobody here – except Tom and Mark, ha ha ha – would want to be a Have-Not. Hands up anyone who'd like to be a Have-Not?' Up shoots my hand. 'There,' he mocks, 'Nobody except Tom. But *I've learned to expect that from you Tom*, ha ha ha…'. a big 'got-you-that-time' glance from the teacher.

'Now hear this – this is the first year that the new Macquarie University is taking undergraduate students. Those of you who aren't good enough to go to a proper university, like Sydney or New South Wales Uni, will wind up there. The best of you will go to Sydney University where I got my teaching qualification. No serious person would go to Tech or Art School, especially not East Sydney Tech, which is full of ratbags. Those secondary-type institutions will be peppered with lower-grade students and time-servers. Time-servers! Now there's a good word for you!'

'Two words,' says Sue, quick as a blink.

'Oh yeah,' he stumbles, 'Time-servers - right. Er…take a flight of fantasy into the new society of the 1980s and 90s and you'll see there'll be no more government assistance schemes, no place for those who fleece society of its assets. I wouldn't want it, would you? Put your hand up if you'd like to receive the dole and see the taxpayer robbed?' Mark whacks his hand up. Devlin ignores im. 'There - nobody. Proof again what a good group we have here.'

'Sssugar, you're right!' whispers Pye to me. 'His fly IS undone!'

I crane my neck, hoping to see right in.

'And sex,' Devlin continues. 'Nowadays it's everywhere. It's painful for moral people to live through these permissive times. Sex sex sex. Everywhere I look I see short skirts, sex magazines, sex on TV, sex sex and more sex.'

Everywhere?

I take a glance around the room, checking out the girls in my class. I - Tom Truscott of Turramurra - have never found it. Cut my thoughts for coconuts. God knows I've looked everywhere for sex and never – well, seldom – found it.

I'm wondering if anyone else has noticed Devlin's fly.

Maybe one of the girls has. Robyn? Janet? It doan seem so. Jenny? Jenny would be really sad about it, especially if it gaped right at her. Janine Turner would be rapt. She'd simply giggle.

'Psst Mark, check is fly…'.

This is great - Devlin's always on at me to keep my shirt tucked in. How come there's rules about shirts but none about flies? I've never heard of a skool that says you've gotta keep your zipper done up otherwise you cop lines.

'Last year...' Devlin continues about sex, '...the front page of the *Mirror* featured a stripper called Sandra Nelson walking through Kings Cross wearing a topless dress designed by a German. These are indeed times of change'.

The times they are a-changin is the expression, man.

'Psst, Ian, his fly's undone.'

'Really?' smiles Ian. Then, remembering he's on the short list for Skool Captain, suddenly gets all responsible and says, 'He's got to be told!'

'You'll spoil it. Look, they're Y-fronts!'

'Y-fronts!' Greg laughs so hard he falls off his chair. Greg is always falling off his chair.

Devlin drones on, back to Hong Kong it seems. 'As soon as a pupil from Hong Kong arrives home, he gets something to eat, then starts straight into his homework, which he doesn't usually finished til midnight.'

'Or she,' says Sue.

He ignores her. 'Greg, what are you giggling about?'

'It's just that your...'

'There's never any excuse for giggling in class. It's the height of bad manners. Unless of course you'd like to share the joke with the whole class, eh?'

'But your...'

'That's the sort of thing I'm up against with you lot the whole time – see? Now what was I talking about?'

'Sex,' says Mark, brushing the hair out of his eyes.

'Is that all you ever think about!' ('Yes' Mark mumbles under his breath.) 'We were *actually* talking about the difference between Hong Kong and Sydney's attitudes to school and how that will affect you all when job-seeking in the future'. The more he waves his arm, the better the view.

He now raves on about 'noble professions'.

Not this again. Argggh.

Anything but the noble professions rant. We cop it every time he runs out of material. Yeah, yeah – noble professions are dentistry, law, architecture, unless you're a girl, then it's back to secretaries and receptionists.

'I'm a bit of a radical amongst my peers,' he prattles on. 'They reckon a woman's place is behind the sink, whereas I think that's only partly true...' Sue is looking pissed off again and I think he said that just to needle her. 'I like to see a woman get behind the switchboard too, to bring in a few shekels to supplement her husband's career...'

Pye gets a big conscience pang, stops doodling and whispers. 'He's got to be told. Really. This guy's representing our school and you can just about see his cock! My mum would freak!'

'Get serious willya, don't tell im!'

'I'm serious Tom, it can't go on...' Pye writes a note to be relayed to Adrian because teachers take Adrian seriously.

The note says, *Tell Devlin his fly's undone.* 'Psst Tom, pass this.'

I pass it to Mark, who passes to Daks, who passes to Janet, who passes to Colin, who is about to pass it to Adrian when Devlin cuts in.

'What's that Colin?' says Mr Expert-on-women-in-society, sex and nose-picking. 'What's that piece of paper?'

'It's a piece of paper,' Colin replies. Ha ha har.

'Stand up and read it to the whole class.'

Teachers love doing this. Always hoping there's a word like fuck in it.

'Ferget it sir, it's nothing.'

'Then if it's nothing boy, let ME read it aloud. Bring it here!'

Colin hesitates, so Devlin strides down the aisle, the gape in his pants grinning eye-height at Janice.

He snatches the note, opens his mouth to commence the Big Read – reddens – spins around, walks back to the chalkboard, fiddles with himself for what seems like ages. Snigger, snigger – that's coming from the class.

When he turns around and faces us, Devlin he's wearing the silliest smile. And for our part, I can't recall our class ever being this quiet. Hmm.

Devlin flicks a look at his wristwatch and seems disappointed. Hmm.

'Er...right...' he tries to pick up the flow. 'What does the 80s and 90s tell you about time-servers who fly – er fleece – society of its assets?'

Silence.

'Greg?'

'What sort of dopey question is that?'

'Beg pardon Greg!'

'I don't get the question...'

'You don't get the question? Leave class immediately. We'll discuss it outside.'

'Sure Mr Devlin,' Greg shrugs. 'Anything you say Mr Devlin.'

And out they go, both of them.

*

There's a long silence, broken by Daks making a farting noise on the back of his hand.

We all laugh and chuck things at him.

I check the time. Ten more minutes before the bell.

'Go on Tom,' says Paul. 'You've now been told to see the Boss about your hair.'

'Yeah yeah yeah, Mr Not-Yet-Prefect,' I leer at him, 'Can't bloody wait fer yer badge can you?'

As I walk out I scribble VOTE PYE in big letters on the chalkboard.

3

Shape of Things

Outside the Boss's office you just sit and wait. Then some smartarse teacher usually wanders past and orders you in a tough voice to 'stand'. So you just stand and wait.

The Boss always keeps us hanging outside, which leaves time to think about the rave he's about to lay down.

It's always the same kinda stuff: cut your hair, you've got a bad attitude, cut your hair, you spend too much time talking to girls, cut your hair, what are you gonna do when you leave skool, cut your hair, why are you wearing elastic-sided boots, cut your hair, take that ring off, cut your hair, you hang around the wrong crowd, cut your hair, you listen to the devil's music, cut your hair, and next time you get sent here I'll suspend you for a week.

'Hello Mr Kennedy,' I say to my Art teacher as he walks past.

'In a bit of…ah…trouble Tom?'

'Yes Mr Kennedy, just a bit.'

'What is it this time?'

'Dunno.'

'How about dropping into the Art Room for a chat some time when you're free?'

'I'll never be free in this place,' I whinge, quickly adding, 'but yes, I'll do that'. He's okay – Mr Kennedy is.

Yawn. What to do while waiting? I dig into my pockets wondering if anything can help pass the time. I find a postcard from Cousin Ken who's being the family hero in Vietnam. It's addressed to Mum and Dad.

Ken is four years older than me and the kind of guy who doesn't mind a barney, while me and my friends are all pacifists. Ken enlisted in the Regular Army as soon as he was old enough. He couldn't wait to go fight in some war like our fathers did.

The weird thing is, apart from him having muscles and me not, he looks more like me than anyone else in the family. We've got the same face.

I pull his card out and read it:

Dear Auntie and Uncle,

At the moment I am stationed just outside Baria which is 128 miles from Saigon. The weather is a great problem to us at the moment as we are in the middle of the monsoon period. It's very hot one moment and the next it pours with rain, and as the area we are camped in is thick red clay, the water does not soak into the ground but lays on the surface causing big muddy puddles. Thinks: why did I join the army?

I remember why.

It was cos when we were kids, his dad and mine sat around the kitchen table drinking Fosters on Sunday arvos. When they weren't bragging about who made the most money that week they'd swap stories about who was the biggest hero in World War II. Ken used to listen to those stories about his old man fighting the Yellow Peril. Not me. I was too busy. I was glued to Little Richard singing. *Awopbopaloobop Alopbamboom.* Awopbopaloobop Alopbamboom made much more sense.

What else have I got?

An ad for the *The Loved Ones Spectacular* coming up at the Trocadero on February 26. Hmm, there's Colin Cook, Ronnie Burns, Lyn Randell, Gus & the Nomads, Ray Hoff & the Off-Beats, the Kinetics and the Cherokees all on the same bill.

Bob Sims walks up and stands beside me. Bob is black – well, half. He's an Abo. A boori. A koori. A choc-drop. A Pidjandjara pisspot. A jungle bunny. A plagon drinker. A bead-buyer. All in all, my kinda of guy.

I know his back story. Bob's ole man is a dinki-di Aussie, a hundred per center. He was a ranger in Alice Springs where he got his Aboriginal wife preggers with Bob. Apart from the other whites ragging Bob's Dad for being a 'gin-jockey', everything worked out fine until Bob's ole lady died from hepatitis. So Bob and his Dad moved to Hornsby where he bought the servo where my ole man buys his juice. After a bit, he re-married, which explains Bob's white younger brother and sister. I don't talk to Bob about his real mum, hep an all that, cos I don't know how to talk about the dead.

The only people who say anything about Bob's colour are some parents and a couple of teachers. Devlin calls Bob a 'fuzzy-wuzzy ha ha ha' on account of his Hendrix hair. But the students don't put any racist bullshit on him. He's too big for the juniors and the seniors all think he's cool. He's not a Spag or a Slope.

Bob – 'What's happening?'

Me – 'Gotta see the Boss. And you?'

'Hair.'

'Me too, must be a clampdown on hair.'

'Yair.'

'Seen any good bands lately?'

'Not since the Missing Links played the Hornsby Police Boys Club and smashed the piano.'

'Dead set!'

'And you?'

Saw the Yardbirds with Page on guitar.'

Cool! Who was the support?'

'Johnny Young.'

'Johnny Young? Ha!'

'But the Yardbirds were fantastic.'

'Of course. Did Page bow it?'

'Yeah, towards the end he pulled out a violin bow. How would that be, playing like that!'

'Try it...' says Bob, '...how's the band going?'

'Aw, ya know...'

'Yair, I got the pitcher.'

'Hey, there's a good Loved Ones gig coming up at the Troc. Why don't you come?'

'Who else is going?'

'Mark, pro'bly with some girl. Plus a coupla guys I don't think you know.'

'Yeah, I don't mind. I'll make it if I don't have to pump petrol.'

Delia, a new girl, walks past. We don't say anything.

'Hey man, how you gonna get out of cutting your hair?'

'Can't I guess,' he concedes.

'Me neither. But Clayton was telling me about a guy – George - at Normanhurst High. He sings in a Normo band called The Mob and got his ole man to write a note saying George needs long hair for income reasons – you know, the band. His headmaster bought it!'

'No shit!'

'Couldn't tell the Boss here that.'

'Can't tell him nuthin. But...how's your band?'

'Aw, not so good...Marto's quit'.

'He was an okay drummer, right?'

'Yair.'

'Why'd he quit?'

'Cos of 6th Form study. His old dear gave him the word and that was it. But he said he'd lend his kit.'

'I had a bit of a tap on it at last year's school fete.'

'I know, I was there...'.

'That's right.'

'You wouldn't consider…?'

'Nah,' he replies, 'Drums are fun, but you know how it is man, I prefer writing songs.'

'Yeah but you could – you know – audition and join our band. We're a running unit and I reckon we can pull some gigs maybe.' My turn to smile.

'I can't join something with a bloody stupid name. What did you call yourselves at that church hall? The *Raspberry Alliance!'*

'Yeah but that was Mark's idea and we only used it once. Like the Strawberry Alarm Clock. Anyway, we're thinking of changing it.'

'Jeez, I'd hate to hear his other suggestions!'

'Look, it's just a name. If we had it together the Mob would let us open for them. Anyway, I've got another name – *The Calculated Guess.'*

'Worse!'

'Okay, NOT the Calculated Guess, I don't mind.'

'I've thought of a name,' says Bob, 'for a band'.

'Whut?'

'You'll only pinch it.'

'I wouldn't. Anyway, you're with me. I'll write words and you write the riffs.'

'Yeah, but I want to play lead and you're sticking me on drums.'

'Look – you can't do guitar, you haven't got a decent amp. We've got a kit that you can play. Either you join a band with equipment or you've got to save up forever to get an amp. We've got some gigs man - the Mob like us. And don't worry about the name. Get your ass over to Jay's place this weekend for a practice – how bout ut?'

Bob thinks for a bit then says, 'What about the other guys?'

'Leave them to me, it's my band.'

'Okay – what about calling it *The Blitz*?'

'*The Blitz Brothers*!'

'No, just *The Blitz*.'

'Okay, I'll run it past the others.'

'I thought you said it was your band?'

'Well, I'm the main lyric writer. How's this for words, I called it *Adum - I am an injection, a handful of sperm cells…'*

'Nice…it rhymes with *smells.'*

'We'll write a few originals together, you & me. Meanwhile I'll get the kit, and we can have a run-thru this weekend, okay?'

'Okay.'

Slam bang crash. Out comes the boss. He drops his papers, shouts instructions to the school secretary, yells at a passing first former, takes a kick at the school dog and glares at Bob & me.

'The Haircut Brigade!' he yells. 'Bob – your black jumper isn't regular uniform. Get into my office!' He reaches for a tug at Bob's hair, which Bob neatly dodges. I listen at the door. I hear him call Bob a worthless, slothful, slovenly disgrace to this proud nation and wonder if he'll come up with new list for me?

My turn next. 'As for you!' He comes up close. I can smell his armpits. 'No pride in yourself! No pride in your uniform! No pride in your schoolwork! No pride in your school! You indecent piece of social flotsam – we should have expelled you long ago. Look at you - you ning-nong! You look like a sissy, you degenerate rebellious delinquent – what are you?'

'An indecent piece of social flotsam,' I reply. 'Oh, and what's a ning-nong?'

'An idiot, like you!' he yells before slam banging the door and crashing into the furniture. Then just as he tells me to get out, back he comes.

'In-cid-ent-ally...what do you know – Tom Truscott – about the graffiti chalked up in the Boy's Toilet – ay?'

'What graffiti?'

'Call me *Sir!* Have you no respect for properly constituted authority? You bedraggled good-for-nothing piece of unemployable teenage refuse! What do you know about this VOTE PYE rubbish?'

YAHRONGA
Lady IN HER
NAKED LUNCH
EAT ME!
YUM YUM
A NORTH SHORE LINE

4

To Sir With Love

I'm not allowed back into class until my hair is short enough, which I think it is now.

But first it's got to be inspected by the Boss. If he's satisfied that I'm sufficiently humiliated he'll write a note to my class-teacher that says yes Tom now looks tame enough to teach.

I've got to be inspected, so I'm hiding for cover.

*

We don't muck up on all teachers. We kinda suss out the fakes, the ones who enjoy punishing us and the ones who are really scared about what we might do next.

Yes, some are actually scared of us. Yep, scared that 'if they give us an inch we'll take a mile'. Scared that if they allow us to whisper in class we'll start yelling and chucking stuff around. Scared that if they let us wear normal clothes that it'll be that much harder to push us around because the youngest of them would look like the oldest of us.

I don't hate every single one of the teachers. I like Kennedy, my Art teacher. I don't mind my Ancient History teacher, Calder. And I might've put up with English if not for my idiot teacher who mocked TS Eliot, the only poet I liked. I never understood why he did that. After Keats, Percy Bysshe and all those odes to bloody butterflies and Grecian urns, ole TS was a fucken relief.

Even though I don't like classroom poetry, I quite like real poetry. I like Adrian Mitchell's *Tell Me Lies About Vietnam.* I like Pete Brown's, 'They slammed the door in my face, I opened the door in my face', and I really like the Mersey Poets. They're like the Beatles in print. Pop poems. Roger McGough's 'arminarmed across the lawn' and 'nuclearage'. One-word spelling like that appeals to me. My dumb teacher hasn't heard of any of these poets. Not int'rested either, which he should be, shouldn't he?

It was Mark who taught me how to write my first poem. He only ever wrote one and couldn't be bothered writing any more. He called it *Positively Mockerism* and at least it relates. It goes:

I wear the clothes I like
I listen to the music I like
I go to bands I like
I read the books I like
I date the girls I like...(I can't remember the rest).

'That's brill!' I told him, 'set it to music and we'll play it in the band!'

'Nah...' he said, 'there's lots of good songs around without writing crook ones'.

Copying his idea for *Positively Mockerism,* I wrote a song to last year's girlfriend Irene, who now thinks I'm a creep. It's my first-ever song and the chords are *Keep On Running* backwards, E-D-A-G. Everyone in the band said it was good, though not good enough to perform in front of an audience. Pissed me right off they did. How can it be one without the other?

Today I decide to spend my free period in the Art room with Mr Kennedy who doesn't come out much but if you make the effort to go see him he always has something good to say.

Like the Woodwork teacher, Mr Kennedy never wears ties. He often paints in the Art room between periods and when I go see him he talks about jazz music and artists. Especially Vincent.

Kennedy had a nervous breakdown some years ago. (We heard that through the grapevine.) I think that's why he stammers a bit. I wish more teachers would have nervous breakdowns if that's what it takes to make someone nice.

*

I go down the stairs lined with student pictures and open the door, 'Hello Mr Kennedy…'.

'Is that you Tom? Come in, I'm sketching.'

'Yep, it's me.'

'How were your holidays?'

I tell him about Jimmy Page, the Walker Bros, Jeff St John and my cousin Ken. Also about Stephanie whose ole man said I mustn't date her. And that I had to get a haircut before being allowed back into class.

'Well…' says Mr Kennedy, who always speaks slowly but means what he says. 'This year of 1967 is…ah…a very important year because…ah…after this you'll be pretty much an adult, maybe getting a job I think p'raps'.

'The Boss told me I'm unemployable.'

Kennedy ignores that and continues, 'Well…what are your expectations for this…ah…year?'

'I haven't thought it through Mr Kennedy. I mean, I haven't yet decided to go to university and BE something or not be something. Just cruisin, I guess.'

'So…1967 – Tom – is…ah…just drifting through to see what turns up?'

'Yeah, is that bad?'

'Things aren't necessarily good or bad. Just different. However there surely must be certain things you wish to…er…achieve?'

'Personal things or job-things?'

'Personal.'

'Oh yeah Mr Kennedy, oh yeah.'

'What are these things?'

'Well, I'd like to learn more about writing songs and more about music and more about playing guitar with a violin bow and more about Art – all for the heck of it, not like for better grades and stuff. Know what I mean?'

'I know what you mean.' Mr Kennedy keeps sketching while he talks but I can't quite understand the sketch.

'I think I'd like to memorise all the notes on the guitar neck so I can find E anywhere and do those boxed finger movements that lead breaks are about. If I could learn a new chord or a new note every day, that's something I'd like to get out of 1967. And I'd like to paint better. An there's lots of novels I'd like to read, like *Catcher in the Rye*. A friend of mine called Salli told me to read it.'

'Hmm,' said Mr Kennedy, 'Is that it?'

'What do you mean, *is this it?'*

'Well...if you don't mind me putting forward a point of view Tom – while your ambitions for 1967 are worthwhile, they're not...um...the kinds of achievement that will...'

'Make money?'

'I'm not thinking about money Tom – you know me better than that – I'm thinking that you need something that will, well...stretch a fellow like yourself. These are the kinds of...ah...achievement that I'd want in *any* year. But the final year of high school is special, it's a defining year that leaves you poised to face your future. So you need more.'

'You mean I need – what? A career?'

'No, a direction. I mean that somewhere in your...ah...outlook, you might like to include something about life itself. Something that goes beyond the chords, the paintings and the...um...novels. These things you should always want for. What you need in 1967 is something that makes you stretch. You need to prepare for the 70s and then the 80s. And, if the world hasn't destroyed itself by then – into the 1990s. Now...ah...while the school *says* it's about preparation for life, it isn't really. That's no secret. Next year you won't be sheltered under this...ah...umbrella.'

'Bloody parents and teachers! They're no shelter!'

'Believe me Tom, they actually *are.* Without them you'd be out in the workforce.'

'I want to go to Melbourne...'

'Not New York, London or Paris? Just Melbourne...er...sure...'

'Mr Kennedy, there are things I wanna do but they're not the kinda things that matter to parents and teachers. I wanna earn deadest real dollars just from the band. I wanna say, *See this $10 note – I earned it through music.* Because the dollars prove it's a real band. I really wanna do that. And maybe in a year, release a single. I'd luv that.'

'I can understand that, Tom.'

'And Mr Kennedy, I'd really like to have – well – it's kinda hard telling this to a teacher – but I'd really like to have my first proper sex. I'm 18 and all my friends reckon they've done it but I haven't. I think about goddamn sex all the time!'

'Well,' says Mr Kennedy patiently. 'I can understand that too. Though I don't think it's necessarily going to be as...er...important as you probably think. But at 18 it's very natural you wanting to find out about...ah...sex. Anything more?'

'And Mr Kennedy, I'd really like to get drunk. The teachers think I do drugs, but I've never smoked marijuana, never dropped acid, never done anything like that. I've been drinking piss since I was 15 - mostly spumante - and I've never bin drunk enough to know what it's like.'

"Well...' says Mr Kennedy. 'I was drunk a long time ago. I did things that made me a bit ah-shamed.'

'Huh?' I didn't know about this.

'Oh, I don't need to say much except that I haven't...ah...touched a drink in 15 years. I go somewhere regularly and still talk to people about it. So I suppose I can understand you wanting to get drunk. But stay away from drugs. You can...ah...expand your mind in other ways.'

'It's quite hip.'

'That doesn't make them less...ah...dangerous.'

'One more thing...' I tell him this because I want him to think I'm 'deep'. Plus I don't want to leave the impression that messing around with drugs is the most important thing to me in 1967. '...I'd also like to understand something that's been worrying me since Grandpa died.'

'What's that?'

'Death.'

I've taken him by surprise. 'Aren't you a bit young to be worrying about that?'

'My friends talk about it a lot, especially Jay whose Dad died when he was 14. I could be dead in Vietnam within a coupla years if I get called up in the ballot. So, what happens after death?'

'Play around with drugs and you just might ah find out!' He snaps. 'Anything else?'

'Yeah Mr Kennedy, I wanna be Hip!'

'Ah gotta talk to you,' he replies with a smile in his voice. 'We gotta talk about Lester Young, Charlie Mingus, Jack Kerouac, the Bebop Babblers and a whole world of jazz. Hip people bug society with attitude, not by drawing attention to themselves all the time.'

The bell rings and he stands up, like all teachers do when a bell rings. 'We were just warming up Tom. I'd really like to keep talking, but ah've got a period coming up. I can see that 1967 will be a big year for you and I've...ah...got some things to read to you that I've never said to you before.' He puts his sketchpad on the bench and I can now see that he's sketching a landscape literally seen through a car window, with the back of the registration sticker on facing in. 'Come back later, I'll have a bit more time around 2.00.'

I quit the Art room and wander around the yard. Maybe I'll spot Delia. I wrote a poem about her last night. Bob might set it to music. But Mark'll only laugh and say 'why write songs when there's so many good ones around already?' He'll point out lines that I call *surrealistic* and say they're rubbish. Lines like, *Peloponnesian vegetarian pillow.* 'It doan make sense' - that's what Mark'll say, the bugger.

*

Everybody's already in class, so I hang around the library and watch Hopkins trying to control form one's Library Period. I wish he bloody would. I came here for a bit of peace.

There's headlocks going on, kids spitting bits of chewed paper through biro plastic while Adrian's little brother is flashing his little dick to the girls who are doing a we-are-so-shocked routine. My god, there's no hope for the younger generation. Hopkins is wimp for not pulling this madhouse into shape. If it's to be, I guess it's up to me.

'Shut up will youse!' I yell, 'I'm trying to read!'

'You wanna make something of it?' squeaks some tiny kid. This kid's all of 13, four foot six and cheeking *ME* out? I'm gonna throttle this idiot.

'What did you just say?' The whole class is suddenly dead quiet.

'Um nuthin.'

'You asked if I wanna make something of it?' Not that I'm tough, but I'm senior.

'Tom! Tom!' Hopkins is bursting across the room, trying now to calm *me* down. I ignore him. Stick with the kid.

'Repeat after me', I tell the kid, '*I am a knob.*'

'I-am-a-knob.'

'Don't let it happen again. Write *Vote Pye* in big letters on your class blackboard – got ut?'

'But you're not a prefect!' his mate joins the act.

'Test me!' I grease him right out.

The second kid lowers his eyes, 'Didn't mean ut'.

Order is restored.

Back at my seat, Hopkins actually thanks me. Then he pulls up a chair and chats to me about stuff like - he's gonna get engaged and then buy a new Holden. I keep repeating, 'Yeah, yeah...great' until the bell tolls. Trouble with him is too goddamn shy to control a class.

*

Eventually I wind up back in the Art room where Kennedy is painting between classes.

'You know Tom,' he begins, 'Your generation owes...um...heaps to my generation, but it won't pay its dues. That's a big mistake in the generation gap...er...as I see it.'

'What do you mean?'

'Well...you see Rock music, for example, wasn't something that started with Presley and peaked with the...er...Beatles. There's a long line of Country Blues that preceded it. I've been wanting to say a few things like this to you and Mark, partly because I think you're interested in this kinda stuff and...ah...also to make you think beyond the pop charts. I don't know much about the new music, but I do know lots about what came before - people like ah Louis Jordan...'

'Who?'

'He sang a great pre-Rock piano boogie called *Caledonia*.'

'I thought Rock n Roll started with Bill Haley?'

'Wrong. If you ever get a chance listen to a guy called Hank Williams - ever heard of him?'

'Nope.'

'Well...er...listen to a song called *Move It On Over* then play *Rock Around the Clock* and you'll see where Haley gets it from. It's practically the same track in the verses, only I like Hank's rendition better. My point is that you kids can't ah-fford to turn the page on the old generation. We set it all up. It was seeded wayback. Take Vincent...'

Having Kennedy as an Art teacher teaches you respect for Vincent as the first Modernist.

Kennedy continues, 'Do you know James Dean?'

'I know he's dead.'

'James Dean played *Rebel Without a Cause* and Brando did *The Wild One*. These are two modern male stereotypes – the Sensitive Loner and the Leader of the Pack. These are the films that started all this teenage stuff.'

'I've seen the Beatles' *Hard Day's Night...'*.

'Sure,' he continues. '*A Hard Day's Night* is fun but it's not important. These other films are. And Juliette Greco - who I'll tell you about another time. I'm just throwing ideas...ah...ah-bout, because if you want to understand present culture – and ah think you do – you've got to understand its...roots.'

'I think I know what you mean Mr Kennedy. Every time Eric Clapton does an interview he always reckons he copies old black Blues players, like BB King.'

'And is this Clapham any good?'

'Him and Jimi Hendrix are the best electric guitarists in the history of the world!'

'Well, the electric guitar has only been around 17 years...you have a lot of promise Tom. It's not that you lack discipline. You'll work for hours, but only if it int'rests you. Ah couldn't squeeze anything out of you on Monet. Yet on Dalí - you came up with an A+ assignment.'

'Yeah – Monet, Manet – that's tea-towel art. They're what Turramurra mums hang in their kitchens.'

'No – that's what they've *become* - but we've argued enough about this enough in class. Anyway, it's from people like me you can learn about the Old Masters, not the Young Masters. From your English teacher you learn your Keats, your Shelley and your Shakespeare. And although you seem to like me better, I'm just like all your other teachers. Just as Mr Bidwell hasn't taught you Allen Ginsberg, I haven't taught you...ah...Warhol.'

'Who?'

'Andy Warhol is probably...er...the most important artist of this period and I haven't even mentioned him.'

'Oh the Campbell Soup guy? Is he any good?'

'He is to Pop Art what the Beatles are to...ah...Pop Music. I don't personally like Pop Art, I prefer the Abstract Expressionists who obscured the image, whereas the Pop Artists made it too obvious. But I like Vincent best of all.'

'Yeah Mr Kennedy, we all like Vincent because of your classes.'

'I've got his...ah...biography somewhere. Would you like to borrow it Tom?'

'Yeah, sometime.'

I watch Mr Kennedy take a pull at his beard, which is showing the first signs of greying.

He says, 'I'm using ochre and yellow because of Vincent. And red because of...er...passion. There's not enough passion in the world Tom. There's not enough love, not enough courage. People aren't enraged enough by injustice. People aren't moved to tears often enough. People don't admire beautiful objects for long enough. We're all too bottled up, too guilt-ridden for our own good. This robs us of our courage and passion!'

'No one really thinks of you as a man of passion Mr Kennedy?'

'Ah...the paintings are where it all goes,' he replies.

Knock knock. In walks Adrian the Sports Hero. 'Excuse me interrupting, but the headmaster sent me to find Tom'. He spots the painting. 'My, what an interesting choice of colour! I guess you'll paint over those ochres?'

'See ya Mr Kennedy,' I shrug. 'And thanks for the talk. I'll think about what you said and maybe borrow that book.'

And off I go with Adrian, to have my hair checked by the Boss.

'I've got quite a good eye for colour,' continues Adrian as we walk along the bloody skool verandah. 'That ochre's quite yuk...'

'Shaddup about the bloody ochre!'

*

I go see the Boss. He says my hair is *just* okay to go to class with. But he'd have liked to have seen it a bit shorter here and a bit shorter there. He reaches his hand to tug the long bits. I withdraw. So he then tries to wrap his arm around my shoulder fatherly-like, but I dodge that too. Sometimes the Boss is all hands.

Weird office. The Queen on one wall and Jesus nailed up miserable and crucified on the opposite wall. Both spend all day staring at each other.

'What are your plans for 1967 Tom?' asks the Boss.

'Just music, I guess.'

'Tell me...' he goes all fatherly now. '...what is Rock Music about Tom?'

'I suppose we're trying to destroy Classical Music. That's what's it's about'. For a fleeting moment I reckon the Queen smiled and the Jesus laughed.

'You! You!...' he reddens, bangs the desk with his fist – ouch – and yells, 'To think...we...tolerated you! I've never heard such nonsense! You scumbag teenage rebel! Listen good...!' His fists are clenched and he's trying to stop them shaking. By god, I musta said summink right.

'Tom Truscott, you're nothing but a destroyer. And you will never, ever, *ever* be a prefect! Get out of my sight!'

'A prefect?'

'Never!'

'Nope, I guess not...' I shrug and make a move towards the door. From his top drawer he pulls a page, which he waves about.

'I've got the list and you're not on it. Adrian is Boys Captain. Jenny is Girls Captain. Colin, Robyn, Peter, Sue, Greg are all prefects...!'

'Mark? What about Mark?'

'Mark? Of course not! Janet, Arnold, John, Sue, Andy...'.

'John...as in John Pye?'

'Yes of course I mean Pye. He got a lot of student votes and the teachers ratified it.'

'Pye!' I can't stop grinning.

'Yes, yes, yes! Now get out, I have to make this announcement public.'

*

I tear out of the office, race down the stairs, collide boom with Miss Dickens – right on her boobs – ooh-ah, sorry – I jump a garbage bin, 'Pye! Pye!'

He's reading *Huck Finn,* which he puts down calmly. He adjusts his glasses and looks up.

'Ee did it ole son! You're a prefect! A fucken prefect!'

'Now Tom, if that's true, you've really got to mind your language when you talk to me. Swearing is against the rules.'

'Goddamn it man, we've bin swearing and splitting and slagging around together for five fucken years!'

'We're not kids any more Tom.'

'I bloody *made* you!'

'What do you mean "made me"'?'

'Vote Pye! Remember *Vote Pye?* Can you remember as far back as last week? What's happenin here?'

'Tom, people didn't go for that graffiti. They voted for the inherent qualities they saw in me as a person...'

'Shaddup!' I grab his shoulder. 'I'm not believing this! We wuz mates only a day ago, we wuz on the same side, man. You can't lay all this leadership stuff on *ME*. You can't suddenly change just cos someone hands you a cheap badge. I'm gonna beat the goddamn shit outta you if you fucken talk to me like that.'

I've got him by the collar now. 'Just don't you ever dob me in Pye. Don't ever, *EVER* give me lines...or I'll smash your teeth in!'

5

My Generation

It's not like me to get upset with Mark and Jay, but they're being mega-unreasonable about Bob joining the band.

Mark says *NOBODY* joins without a proper audition. And then there's the name-change to *The Blitz*, which he reckons isn't on either.

'You don't get it guys,' I tell them, 'I've worked everything out!'

'Great, then you don't need us,' says Jay.

'Ang about! Wivvout a drummer we haven't got a band. We're a nothing!'

This is all being said at Jay's house in Gordon and the four of us – Mark, Jay, Bob and me are sitting around in Jay's room, which is the garage out the back. (Bob's not saying a word.)

All over the floor there's our stuff – a drum kit in bits, lyric sheets, guitar leads, gaffa tape and the mike stand I painted pink for an Art assignment. I called it *Mike Stand* and got a B.

On Jay's walls there's a gold and red Dylan poster by Martin Sharp and a poster of Zappa, trousers down around his ankles, sitting on a dunny and looking mean. (Jeez, I wouldn't wanna cross im.)

Bob is looking at those walls and not saying much, wondering pro'bly how come I didn't sort out this band stuff before, so he wouldn't have to hear all this.

'Listen,' I tell Mark, 'I started this band and I want Bob IN!'

'Okay, if it's YOUR band, you and Bob can both piss off and do whatever you like together.'

'No…I didn't mean ut like that. It's your band too - an Jay's. I thought you'd be grateful. I've come up with a drummer!'

'Well how about giving us a fucken say in what's goin down…!'

'You get heaps of say Mark. You and Jay pick all the songs. You doan consider anything I've written. You doan even let me play guitar much anymore!'

'We did let you play…' now Jay joins in, '…and when you did, you played *Satisfaction* faster and faster until no one could keep up. It was awful. You're welcome to play any time you decide to play properly.'

'But I like playing fast. You've got to play *Satisfaction* fast otherwise it's boring.'

I fight with my mother, I fight with my father, I fight with my teachers, I fight with the Boss, I fight with my girlfriends and here I am fighting my band.

(Well…obviously not exactly MY band.)

'Look Tom,' says Mark. 'We've been mates since we've been 14. I'd rather stick the band and stay friends.'

'The band is what we're friends for! Can't drop it now we've got a drummer and a gig!' Mark starts combing his hair. He gets away with way longer hair than me an Bob, cos Mark's hair is straight and therefore naturally neat - even when long. 'I can't have a band without you Mark. How come everything's so bloody difficult?'

Bob's still watching all this.

Jay answers, 'What you're doing wrong Tom is - you're doing your own bloody thing and expecting us to fit in around you. Like that fucken song to Irene you wrote. You keep saying we ought to play it just cos you wrote it, but that's not enough of a reason. It's also gotta be good. But Mark...' Jay takes a different tone, '...Tom's right about the name mate. We've got to change it and I think *The Blitz* is a great suggestion.'

'I'm not against the name change,' says Mark. 'And I've got nothing against Bob. All I'm saying is that no one – not Tom – not anyone – does anything without all of us agreeing. Audition first. That's how it's done. That's what being a group is about'.

Bob's a patient sort of guy.

He doesn't take any of this personally. He just watches the argument like a tennis match. Fifteen-love. Fifteen-all. Thirty-15. It might be match point now - so long as I don't remind them of *Satisfaction*.

'C'mon then,' says Jay. 'Let's sort the gear and have a bit of a play.'

To Bob he says, 'Sorry mate, I'm not trying to be a bastard and it's nuthin against you.'

We know that Bob won't stuff up the audition.

He'll be in the band now for sure.

Plus, I reckon we'll definitely change the name. So I bite my lip and cut my thoughts.

'Let's play some fucken music!'

'But Bob's not singing Tom,' Mark adds as an after-thought.

'Why not?'

'Because we agreed that drummers never...! Shit Tom! Oh never mind, let's just set the gear up. Did you remember to bring the song list?'

'Yep,' I reply (cos I often forget).

Phew.

THE LOVE
GODESSES
Leave HIM alone YOU Bitch!
Do YOU LOVE ME GODESS?
The world is but a silver screen and we are but actors playing
WITH a T.
or BARDOT
or GARBOT

6

Sunshine Superman

'What's it gonna be then, eh?'

Black espresso ex-presso thanks, plus two cappuccinos and a white. Coffee – that's the newest thing. Here, they make the cappuccino on Instant Coffee. Everything's Instant. But I still feel like a coffee-house Beatnik in Soho. What did Kennedy say about Mingus?

The Turramurra Milk Bar is next to the Commonwealth Bank building, through the Turramurra Park (The Tuz) and across the Pacific Highway from the station. It's our hangout. Sort of, after-school Zen with Bob, Mark and Jay.

Let me tell you O my Blitz Bruvvers that to our left drinking fruit juice and chewing gum I have spotted three PLC girls who have definitely eyeballed us. If they could only be told we are not what we seem (Jay usually carries his guitar around everywhere!) they might arsk our true identities and discover that we are not ordinary sixth formers but lo the fabulous Blitz - songwriters and poets with a deep and sensitive understanding of the Liverpool and Sydney underground sound.

The beautiful one with the Byrds granny-glasses and a flower behind her left ear I claim as mine, cos I saw her first. Never have I fallen so quickly in luv.

I don't confess this to my mates, in case they've got their own fantasies. But for her, I'd cross the Milk Bar floor and say, 'G'day my name is Tom, can I buy you another frozen orange juice?' I bet Mark is thinking similar, but more evil, thoughts. Damn. He's combing his hair again.

Clayton will be along soon - and Salli, who I am supposed to be meeting. I hope she doesn't show up quite yet.

It's from Salli that I get my best ideas.

There's something down-to-earth about her. She's in Fifth at Hornsby Girls High.

It was Salli who introduced me to BB King and John Lee Hooker. It was Salli who gave me the confidence to grow long hair, even though mine's curly. It was Salli who told me about the Beats – Ginsberg, Corso, Ferlinghetti and LeRoi Jones. Salli lent me the Fugs record. Salli likes my poems. Salli encourages me to write songs. Salli lent me the money to buy the elastic-sided boots that drive the Boss around the twist.

But Salli is a problem because it's Salli's expression of disgust I see whenever I try to pick up little skoolies who look like they belong at a Johnny Young concert. She calls them *Bubblegummers.*

Salli reckons I'm very easily led.

Salli sez Mark is *teenybopperbait* and a *SwinGer*. Not a *Swinger*. She sez *Swing-Ger*. Just a pretty boy. She sez I shouldn't be seen dead hanging around a guy who looks like the lead singer of the Monkees.

Salli hates Jay too because she sez he 'uses' women and boasts about what he used them for. Plus he drinks too much.

Salli sez the only two friends I've got who are worth a pinch of shit are Bob (cos he's 'deep') and Clayton who she reckons is 'incredibly mature' because he doesn't mind a chat about the soul, the Rainbow Serpent and god, etc. Everywhere he goes Clayton carries a Marine Band blues harp, which he doesn't play and a copy of *Ulysses* by James Joyce, which he never reads. No wonder they reckon he's mature.

It is this very Salli who I am waiting for now - the main obstacle to me crossing the milkbar and chatting up the blonde wearing Jim McGuinn/Byrds glasses.

So here we all are, drinking Turramurra coffee, eating Turramurra toasted cheese-and-tomato sandwiches, about to pick up three Turramurrans (I hope) when in walks Dad.

'What are you likely lads doing here?' he says, rubbing his hands together all businesslike.

'Waiting for Clayton and Salli,' I reply, quickly stubbing out my fag. Too late.

'Hello Mr Truscott,' says Mark.

'Hello guys,' he smiles curtly at Mark, Bob and Jay. Then to me he says crossly, 'I don't give you pocket money to spend on smokes!'

'Mark's paying. What are you so upset about?'

'Cos you're faggin again!'

'You smoke too…!'

'Sure, but I'm not 18, not in school uniform and I use my own money. I don't pay all these school fees to see you suspended for smoking!'

'That only happened once…'.

Dad flashes a dark look, turns to the counter, orders a packet of Rothmans (obviously why he came here). 'See you back home. Not too late I hope!'

'Okay.'

On his way out he pauses, smiles awkwardly and outs his small change. 'Here you go. Have a good time. And pay Mark back.'

'Thanks Dad.'

Again he looks anxious, then he spills it, 'I…er…had to leave the office a bit earlier than usual today,' says Dad, plucking out a cig then rummaging through his pockets unable to find his lighter. Mark offers his. ('No thanks.')

'…er…Mr Tuktens died, I thought you should know in case you run into his daughter at the station…'

'Who?'

'Mr Tuktens, our neighbour - four doors down.'

'Oh, the old guy you play Bridge with?'

'He was only 48.'

'How'd ee cark it?'

'I beg your pardon?'

'How'd he die?'

'Your language is shocking Tom.' Dad's still trying to find that lighter. 'Your mother thinks it was a heart attack.'

After he leaves Jay pipes up. 'Not a bad sort...your ole man.'

'I hate im.'

'Hate yer Dad! You're bloody lucky you've got one! You shouldn't talk that way about your ole man you dumbfuck. You shouldn't say you hate im not even if yer kidding. Gave you all his change, he did!'

'Two bucks. Big deal. He hates my hair, hates my music, hates everything I do.'

'Doesn't seem to hate it that much. You wouldn't have a bloody geeetar, cept he paid for it...' omigod – Jay's now got a crackle in his voice – '...well, I wish I still had an ole man!'

'Hope I die before I get like my parents,' I exclaim.

'You *don't* wanna die man!' Jay yells, 'There's no comeback. It sounds hip in a song, but no one really wants to be deadmeat!'. Jay turns to Bob, 'What do you think about all this bullshit Bob?'

'I know what you mean Jay...', is all he says. And I suddenly remember that Bob's Mum died too.

'Well fame never dies,' I'm taking them all on now. 'We still study Napoleon – so he's still alive in a way. And James Dean...!' I continue, over-reaching.

'Who's James Dean?' says Mark. 'Ah-hah, gotcha!'

Then, right outta the blue - 'Is it a boy or is it a girl?' some shorthair who just breezed in-and-out of the Milk Bar yells that at us.

Jay chases after im out on the pavement, '*Brown shoes don't make it, man!*' he shrieks top-of-his-lungs, to puzzled commuters walking past with briefcases.

*

O well, nothing else to do now but make my move on the girls. I cross the floor where their conversation is in full flow.

'...we used every brand of tester perfume in the shop until a guy came up and said *Those aren't testers,* so we beat it...'

'Hi, my name is Tom.'

The two I'm not interested in start giggling. 'She's Bronwyn, I'm Narelle,' says the Tester-Perfume Kid.

Yeah great. 'What's hers?' – meaning the one wearing Byrds glasses.

'It's Samantha – Samantha Evans.'

I check her out, impressed. 'Well, I'm Tom and I'm in a band with these other guys. If ever you want to hear some good music – we play songs by the Easybeats, the Who, Them, the Manfreds, the Loved Ones, the Throb – even a couple by the Fab Four.'

'The Fab what?' says Samantha, with a slight American accent.

'The Fab Four, you know – the Beatles.'

'Oh.'

'We've got a gig coming up. Come along an I'll see you get door passes. We write our own material sometimes, but not always because we want to keep the musical standard mega-high'.

'What's your name?'

'The Blitz.'

'I've never heard of the Blitz,' says Samantha gently touching her lovely blonde hair. 'But I've been out of the country for two years. Have you girls ever heard of the Blitz?'

'Yeah,' says Bronwyn, edging a little closer. 'I've seen the name written in the Waitara Station tunnel...'

'That's us!' I exclaim, rapt to be recognised.

'...or maybe it was The Mob?'

'Yeah, the Mob!' says Narelle.

'No, no...' I insist, 'it was the Blitz!'

'You'd know...' says Samantha, '...you probably wrote it yourself.'

'Yes, but I was hoping you'd write the next one.' Slick, huh?

'What do you want?' says Samantha, 'My Daddy'll be along soon so hurry up.'

'Your who?' I haven't heard anyone say 'daddy' since I turned seven.

'She always calls him *Daddy*,' says Narelle, and by way of explanation adds, 'Samantha lives in Billyard Avenue Wahroonga.'

What am I supposed to say to that? So I add, 'We might be taking the band to London next year...'.

'What's so good about London?'

'Er...only the London Scene!' Ha!

'That was two years ago. If you want a scene, try San Francisco. That's where I've come back from. When I was living in Marin County I'd catch a cab to Haight-Ashbury all the time. Haight-Ashbury was a groove – posters, beads, Indian raga music, comix...*everything.* And the best bands, like the Grateful Dead, Moby Grape, Janis Joplin, Jefferson Airplane, I'd see them all the time.'

'Sorry, I've never heard of them,' I laugh in her face.

'Get this creep outta here!' snaps Samantha, dismissing me with a wave of her hand.

'I've heard of Moby Grape,' says Mark (liar!) overhearing and joining in.

'They're outta sight,' says Samantha plucking a flower from behind her ear and handing it to *him.* 'I've seen them *heaps.* I used to even go to their rehearsals.'

'Yeah?' says Mark.

'Yeah,' says Samantha.

Yeah-yeah-yeah-yeah-yeah-yeah-yeah to everything she says. Yeah what a bloody boring conversation. 'Tell me about yourself, your dreams and your phone number,' I hear him croon.

Then Narelle starts talking to me, 'You guys really a band?'

'Sure, not just a garage band – we play the traps...'

'Like where?'

'Oh, St John's Church Hall once...'

'Really? Where else?'

'Parties...a 21st...nearly played a wedding. But we're really holding ourselves back and rehearsing because we're trying to get that full-on R&B sound.'

'Well, I don't listen to *old* music', she really is a pain, that Samantha.

'Whaddaya mean *old!'* I hate her. 'I saw the Yardbirds four weeks ago. I saw fucken Jimmy Page!'

'Well,' Samantha replies, not even slightly ruffled, 'I like Moby Grape and I don't like you. And I can tell by your language you don't give a shit about Peace & Love.'

*

Speaking of peace & luv, Clayton turn up. He walks in smiling with a copy of *Ulysses* under his armpit. 'Hey Clayton!' I hail him, leaving the girls' booth. Clayton's eyes instantly fix on Samantha but I draw him back to Bob and Jay, leaving Mark to work his magic, the bastard. I saw her first.

'I've brought a friend,' says Clay, looking around for the person he thought was behind him but isn't. 'He must be parking the car – oh, here's Stu now.'

The first thing I notice about Stu is that he's nothing like a Hippie or a Mod. Short hair, a tatt on his right arm ('Mum's Worry') and he's short but built like a brick shithouse.

'Stu's just come up from Melbourne. He lives up the Cross.'

'Don't you go to skool?' I ask.

'Fuck skool!' he replies, staring too long at Bob, cos he's black (I think).

'Jay's quit skool too…', I quickly add.

'Stu got in trouble with the cops last night,' says Clayton.

'What'dya do wrong?' Jay grins. He likes it.

'I did this vicious burnout on the road and they gave me a hard time. I was blind drunk of course…'

'A what burnout?'

'A *veeecious* burnout. How bout moving over so I can sit down?' Shuffle shuffle. Another espresso-expresso. Two more cappuccinos.

'Yeah, this veeecious burnout at the lights. Nearly rolled it too when they took off after me', then Stu cases the joint and says, 'What are we doing in a fucking Milk Bar? Let's go somewhere closer to the city.'

'Where?'

'Luna Park maybe. Hey, is that longhair one of ours?' Stu points to Mark.

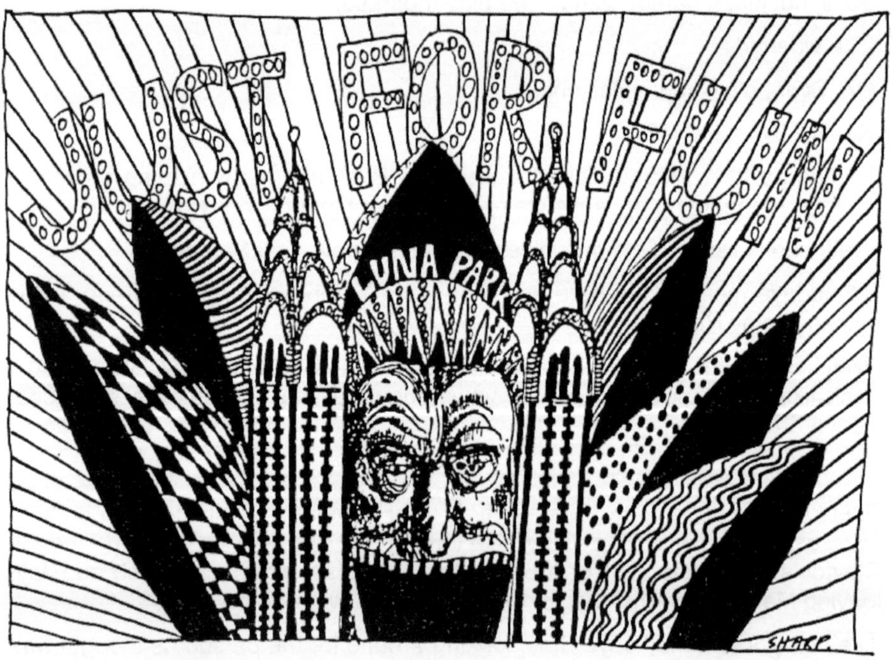

'Yair.'

'What's he up to?'

'What's it look like?'

'Grab im and let's go. Do you guys smoke?'

'Yeah sure...'

'I mean grass fuckhead.' I've only just met this guy and he's already taken charge. 'Hey Blondielocks!' That's Mark he's calling to. 'Got any weed?' Everyone in the Milk Bar is shocked into silence.

'I'm gonna like this bloke,' whispers Jay, understanding that Stu is doing it only for effect.

'Are you kiddin...!' I mutter.

'I smoke weed!' Samantha perks up, unashamed.

'Good – bring her along. I can squeeze seven into the car. Let's just get the fuck outta here.'

'Language! Boys! Boys!' the proprietor's 23-year old son Tony asserts.

'Bloody wog!' Stu spits back, crashing the chair as he walks out. As for me and Bob and even Clayton, we kinda slide out of the joint with lowered eyes. We don't need bad vibes, man.

Samantha strikes it up with Stu and she walks out with one arm around Stu, the other around Mark. 'I've just got to call Daddy first...' she mentions out the door.

'Clayton,' I whisper, 'what the hell's going down?'

'Just this I guess.'

'Where'd you dig Stu up from?'

'I just met him, he passed me a joint and next thing I remembered was I had to meet you guys here.' We both race back to the Milk Bar to pick up the *Ulysses* he left on the seat. This gives us a chance to apologise properly.

'He call me Wog!'

'We don't know him...really!' Clayton and I are trailing the pack now – which is Narelle, Bronwyn, Mark, Samantha, Stu, Jay and Bob. As we cross the railway bridge into Rohini Street I suddenly hear my name.

'Tom!'

*

It's Salli.

'Where've you bin? I've been waiting at the Station an hour!'

'I thought I said the Milk Bar...'.

Then she spots the girls. 'Picking up Bubblegummers were we?'

Samantha spins around, 'I don't take crap from anyone!'

'A pack of kids!' answers Salli. At this point Clayton wisely vanishes. In fact, everyone walks away from Salli and me.

'Picking up 15-year olds to feed your ego isn't my idea of I-wanna-be-an-artist-god-I'm-so-sensitive!'

I wanna crawl away. 'Don't be like that Salli. Come with us to Luna Park.'

'Oh nice - you've somehow blown it with them, so you're asking *me*. There's NO WAY.'

'What's eating you Salli?'

'I know you Tom. I see it all - Jay's gonna get rotten drunk and spew. You'll *tell everyone* you were drunk when you weren't. Mark'll be in the backseat with that tart. The other five of you will spend the night fighting over the other two. Bob'll stay straight and drive everyone home without a license. Thanks but no thanks Tom, I waited for you an hour, now I'm going home. Who is that Stu-guy anyway?'

'Is this all because you waited at the station?'

'Tomorrow you'll be back to I-wanna-be-a-highminded-poet. Get stuffed Tom Truscott!'

It's bad, I reckon, when a friend thinks you're an idiot.

'Go on without me guys, I'm going to hang here with Salli.'

'There's no room for you anyway!' laughs Stu. He's got his arm around Bronwyn.

Samantha is warming to Mark.

Clayton's gonna drive.

Jay is asking Narelle if she's got enough money to buy a hip flask.

And Bob is by himself.

7

Have You Seen Your Mother Baby, Standing in the Shadow?

'No eggs! No eggs! Whaddya mean no eggs!'

'It's not my fault Tom, your Dad ate them all.'

'Damn.'

'What can I do? I can't *lay* them for you', says Mum. 'And don't swear, I don't know what I'm going to do with you boy. One day you'll be the death of me.'

'Everyone over 30 ought to be dead anyway, I reckon.'

'Don't you talk like that to your mother! I'd have never talked like that to my parents. I'm ashamed to have you as a son. I can't believe today's kids! Ava go at that longhaired friend of yours…!'

'Would that be Jay…or maybe Clayton, Bob, Mark…?'

'The one who swore at his mother.'

'Oh…Jay.'

'What's going to become of you kids when it comes time for you all to get jobs?'

'I'm already a poet, singer and artist.'

'You're none of those things. You're a schoolboy and you're *my boy.* While you're living under my roof you'll curb your tongue. Why did you say that ridiculous thing to your little sister yesterday…?'

'What ridiculous thing?'

'That if she didn't behave herself the whole family would gang-spank her? She cried for two whole hours after you went out.'

'Cried five minutes more like. It was just a joke Mum. Jilly's my l'il sis, I'll talk to her how I like.'

'Not while I'm washing your clothes and cooking for you, you won't!'

'Then I'll leave home – like Stu.'

'Oh that's a new one. Who's Stu? A pillar of the community? Someone decently employed? Or just another longhair?'

'He hasn't got long hair. I'm not sure what he does, but he's gotta have a job to pay his rent. He left Melbourne and came to Sydney. I might leave Sydney and go to Melbourne.'

'Where in Sydney, does he live?'

'Kings Cross.'

'I might've guessed!' The kettle boils and Mum gets about making herself the evening Lan Choo. Everything's habit with her. At 7.20 precisely she boils the kettle so that at exactly 7.25 she'll have a nice cup of tea for Dad after kissing him hello on the cheek the minute he walks through the door.

Then it all comes back to her. 'Of course I remember your friend Stu – isn't he the one who did donuts on the council strip and ran over the Royal Highness Roses next door? Not satisfied, he actually kicked his own car. Kicked it!'

'Well no…er, that was Jay again, actually.'

'Stu is one of those *hippies* I suppose.'

'Hippies don't run over roses. They care about flowers. They'd put me up free in a crashpad. They doan believe in capitalism, unlike your lot.'

'…who are generous enough to give you pocket money, pay for your ridiculous clothes and buy you a guitar!'

'Aw Mum, doan be so hard.'

'Yes,' she continues, 'I know all about hippies. I saw these people on the News – naked. *Naked Tom!* They then proceeded to say how good for you LSD is! One even proposed piping LSD into the city water mains so that everyone could get it on tap! He was so environmentally-minded that he gave some to his dog! Is this what we brought you up to believe?'

'At least they believe in love.'

'Don't I believe in love?' exclaims Mum. 'Have you ever contemplated loving your parents?'

'I do love you Mum!' Goddamn. How'd she squeeze that one out of me? 'I love you like any kid loves parents. But you're against everything we do.'

'I put up with a lot. I put up with pictures of that ugly band stuck to your bedroom wall!'

'The Rolling Stones?'

'You've got them pinned up as if they're something to be admired. Yet on the News we heard they were arrested for urinating against a wall!'

'The Stones are old-hat. I'm putting up pictures of Moby Grape and Bob Dylan instead. I hope you like them better.'

'All this trouble started with the Beatles. Nowadays they just don't have nice people in music any more – like Benny Goodman and Bing.'

'You won't have to worry about the Beatles any more either. They've stopped touring.'

'Good.'

'They've played their last concert and when bands stop performing – next thing, they bust up. So you won't have to worry too much about them.'

‘I’ll cook you a steak, boy…’ she says, thinking of other stuff now the Beatles sound over.

‘Was *Bewitched* funny tonight?’

‘It’s always funny, especially that neighbour. And they don’t use bad language like that Alf Garnett.’

‘I like *Bewitched* Mum, so there ya go – something we both like.’ Struth! I just squeezed a smile out of Mum. But behind the smile I see – or think I see – tears. Big sigh. She sits on the nite-n-day and pulls out a crumpled letter. ‘I’ve just received this from your Cousin Ken. He’s not too happy in Vietnam and I think you should hear what he has to say.’ She unfolds it and prepares to read aloud.

‘I’m not in’trested in Ken. I hate war.’

Nevertheless you should hear it, because it might make you think about the real world.’

‘I’m scared I might get called up. I think about Vietnam all the time.’

Quite suddenly an embarrassing loud sob slips out of nowhere. ‘You don’t even know where Vietnam is!’ She sobs a bit then goes back to the letter, reading aloud:

‘Dear Auntie and Uncle,

This is your long lost nephew speaking. How are you all keeping back home in the civilized country? If you ever thought we were uncivilized people in Australia, just come to Vietnam.

‘As you may remember, my posting was for Saigon. I stayed there two weeks and then I was sent to Vung-Tau where there was trouble with our soldiers in the town itself and the Mayor of the town wanted three MPs to keep Australian soldiers and the Australian RAAF in order.

‘Vung-Tau is the leave centre for our troops. It is 11 miles from the front line and consists of 236 bars, 40 massage parlours and a few shops. We used to combine patrols with one American MP, one Korean MP and one Vietnamese MP. Our main duties being checking bars, traffic accidents, investigations of theft, rape, arson, black-market and we also enforce curfew 2330 hours. So as you can see we were kept busy…’

‘Mum…’ I interrupt. ‘I really don’t care about Ken.’

She ignores me and reads on:

‘Whilst in Vung-Tau we averaged 4-6 hours sleep per night and the rest of the time we were on duty. We have not really had much trouble except for two shootings and a hand grenade incident which killed nine people and wounded 13 when it was thrown into a bar a few nights ago…’

‘Mum! This is awful!’

She continues: *'As you probably read in the papers a few days ago, Ian Brown, an MP from Sydney who came up with me was killed by a sniper seven days ago, so once again I was on the move again, up to the front. I am now stationed with the Task Force situated at Nui-Dat in the Phen-Toc province. Just to make us all happy we are in the middle of the monsoon season, so we spend all day walking around up to our knees in mud.'*

'Mum, knock it off!'

'Do you think I'm enjoying this Tom? These are the sorts of letters I was getting from your father in the War, wondering from day-to-day if he was alive.'

I quickly eyeball Ken's letter. It's got a red and yellow crest on each page with the words 'US Forces – Republic of Vietnam' at the top. I chuck it on the coffee table.

'We don't want to encourage these military types. I wrote about Vietnam. I wrote a poem – it goes:

Tear down your cenotaph in Martin Place
We don't want your murdering heroes
You who fight in Vietnam
You who used to kill the negroes…'

She looks at me with contempt. 'Aggh! Don't ever recite that within earshot of your Dad. And I hope to god Ken never sees that!'

Then she picks up Ken's letter and stares at it, as if it might contain some grain of hope. She hasn't read it all yet. Either way, I don't give a stuff, *Til Death Do Us Part* is about to start.

'That's my sister's boy Tom, and we're never sure whether every letter from him mightn't be his last.'

I know her. I know she wants me to put my arm around her. She'd like to have a good cry on my shoulder, but she won't cry in front of me, not now. She reads on, as if there is something in these pages she hopes might teach me something.

'You've probably read in the paper that Ian Brown…'

'You've read that already. I don't need it twice…'

'For chrissakes Tom!' she exclaims, then goes on…

'Our main job at Nui-Dat is traffic control points, convoy escorts, control of all Viet Cong suspects and Viet Cong prisoners, the only difference between the two being the suspects are tied with string and the Viet Cong are tied with barbed wire.

'We also work with Intelligence in regards to interrogations. You may think that the Viet Cong are being treated a bit rough from what you read in the papers but if you could see the remains of the bodies of Australian or American troops like we do – when of course there is enough to bring back – you would have no pity for these people.

'Yesterday the Viet Cong went to a Vietnamese village three miles from our headquarters and slit the stomach of a five-year old girl and hacked the arms off an eight-year old boy so that they could entice our doctor down to the village.

'Intelligence, realizing it was a trap, stopped the doctor from going to the village. The body of the little girl was then staked out in the middle of the road until she died. Enough of the troubles of this nasty world. How are you all keeping?

'Is Grandma as fit as I expect? Did Tom receive his Christmas present I sent him? I would like to thank you both once again for the $300 loan. I am sure I would have been lost without it. You tell Tom from me that if he ever gets the idea about joining the Army – he's mad. All my love – Ken.'

'Join the bloody Army? He must have rocks in his head! I'm gonna watch telly.'

She removes herself from the room, wondering why the hell she bothered reading the bloody letter to me in the first place. Bugger, I can't enjoy the TV show knowing that she's shut her bedroom door and is in there probably bawling her eyes out.

You're playing it wrong Tom Truscott.

You're turning Peace & Love into a hard game.

LOVE
HATE

8
Rock N Roll Music

I suppose you all wanna know where all our dumb houses are. I'll tell you, then the boring bit's up an done.

You know the big *Farmers Department Store* on the corner of Pacific Highway and Dumaresq Street Gordon? Well Jay's family lives down Dumeresq in a brand new house. Before that his whole family lived up the back in the garage that's now Jay's room, while the old weatherboard place was ripped down and this brick veneer update was put up. His old man did the construction. That is, before he got crook.

Mark and I actually live real close to each other. He lives in *Turramurra Gardens* a block of flats on the corner of the Pacific Highway & Duff Street Turramurra. And I live half way down Duff, at the bottom of that steep hill, near Allan Avenue.

Bob – now our official drummer – lives three suburbs away, handy (like us) to the station. Bob lives in Waitara Avenue just opposite Waitara Park in Waitara. It's all Waitara Waitara Waitara for him. It's like when they named the suburb they couldn't spell Wahroonga right.

These suburbs are on Sydney's North Shore and the Westies think our parents are richer than they really are. Mark's parents drive a new Morris 1100. Jay's Mum's got a brand new Holden. Bob's Dad's got about six vehicles cos of the garage business – two old utes, an old Falcon, a newish truck and a Holden Premier X2.

My ole man drives a secondhand Merc.

But we always dress well. I spend all my pocket money on records and clothes. And cigs. We mostly buy our gear from the *In Shop* in Hunter Street, opposite Wynyard Station or *John & Merivale* near Martin Place. When we can't afford to buy clothes, we fix our own. Three years ago Mark figured out, and taught us, how to sew. One of us had to work it out because none of our ole dears would peg our trousers, so Mark figured out how we could do it ourselves. Whenever you get a new piece of skool uniform, it's important to bend it.

Back to Dumaresq Street.

*

Jay's house is right up the front of the block and although he could have had a bedroom in the new place, he prefers to live in the garage. Anyone would. It's real good, with a shower/toilet, small kitchen, plus big car space where our band practices.

I arrive there. 'Where's Jay?'

Mark looks up from tuning his guitar and gestures with his thumb, 'In there – hungover'.

His bedroom door opens. Jay staggers out, 'Gotta cig?' He grabs one. 'Coffee anyone?' He plugs the jug in, looks around for cups, sugar and the Bushells. Then he sits beside us, rolls his head around and says, 'Phew.'

'Everything all right?'

'He came off his motor bike last night,' says Mark.

'Oh I'm all right. Don't listen to Mark. It had nothing to do with the bike.' He points. 'Bike's over there. I never even took it out.'

'Then why'd you say…?'

'That's what I told Mum. Oooh, my head…'.

'What really happened?'

'He was with Stu…' says Mark.

'Yeah, the madman,' Jay pours the hot water into cups as he speaks. 'Blind drunk. We'd been to…I forget where we'd been…'.

'Bronwyn and Narelle,' reminds Mark, looking for the hairbrush

'That's right, we went to see Bronwyn and Narelle. How'd you know?'

'Samantha told me.'

'Samantha phoned *you?*'

'We've been in touch since the Luna Park night.'

'You sly dog,' Jay grins. 'Well that's more than can be said for Bronwyn and Narelle, those bloody sluts hate us now.'

'What happened?'

'Narelle called me an animal for throwing up. And Bronwyn? Well, I'm not sure what went wrong with her and Stu, but things got a bit ugly. Anyway, last night Stu said we should go find Clayton, so we went round to his place and he'd gone out…'

'He was with us.'

'So that's where he was?' Jay ashes his cigarette into his coffee and drinks it anyway. 'So off me and Stu go – to the Greengate, where we drink for a coupla hours. Then Stu said he'd drive me home. It was bonus. But the cops didn't appreciate it, heh heh…' he smirkles.

'They must've watched us go past. I think we were hiking – vvvvm. The big FJ with six different coloured guards. Ya know – bald tyres, screaming along the highway, then Stu pulled the handbrake. All you have to say to im is HANDBRAKE and he instantly reacts. So we did the Big 180 – facing the wrong way, then we saw the Police car coming *towards* us. And we're in the wrong lane!' He lights another smoke.

'After that they pulled us over and asked what happened? Stu said "My brakes locked up". And they bought it. The young copper (cos there was an old Sarge and a young copper – classic, you know). The young guy comes racin out. He had his hand on his truncheon and said, “Keep your hands where I can see them”. I said, “What is this, *The Untouchables* or something?” (You know – something smart-arsed, cos I’d had a few too many and wasn’t the driver.) Then they checked out Stu and the old cop says, “I think you might be over the limit…”. So I started really givin it to them. I was drunk, but only the passenger – you know. And the old guy says to Stu, “Tell your mate to shut up willya”. Stu says, “I can’t tell him to shut up. I’m not responsible for him. He’s a big boy.”’

‘How’d you all finish up?’

‘Well, we were only just up the road from here. They asked Stu where he lived and he pointed to my house. They said, “All right – see’y later then”. And Stu went back to town I guess. He wanted to keep raging, but I was completely fucked.’

‘Jeez mate, you were pretty lucky!’ I tell im.

‘Born lucky.’

‘What about the girls?’

‘God mate,’ says Jay, picking up his guitar, ‘I told you what they called us. No way…hey, are we having a play or whut? Wanna beer?’

‘Too early,’ I answer.

‘Same,’ says Mark.

‘Where’s Bob?’

‘He’ll be along soon,’ I reply, fixing another coffee. ‘He’s got a girlfriend you know…?’

‘So whut’ve you been up to?’

‘Well, I went to Guitar City in Wynyard,’ I reply. ‘You should see the Strats, Teles and Jazzmasters. They also had a Gibson Firebird! I swear I’m gonna save up and buy one. It’s the best lookin axe, man.’

‘What did you say about Bob?’

‘He’s got a girlfriend now…’

‘Who?’

‘Someone he met on the train ages ago.’

‘Oh?’ Jay loses interest, ‘Are we having a play or whut?’

‘How’s yer head?’

‘I’m fine. Are you disappointed that I’m not in pain? Pass me another beer.’

‘Okay, let’s get on with somethin,’ I start organizing the practice. ‘The gig’s not far off now, so I wanna throw an idea at you. Stop playing a minute Jay. C’mon – concentrate.’ I switch off his amp.

‘Oh thanks Tom, that’s what my mother would do…’.

'Yeah, sorry. Look. I've come up with an idea for a cut-up song. I got the idea from Salli actually...'

'That bitch,' says Mark.

'Don't talk about her like that!' I get upset when Mark bags her out and when she bags him. 'Give this a go at least. I took *Eve of Destruction* and a poem by TS Eliot and cut them up, put the lines in a hat, drew them out line-by-line and that's how I did the words. Just give it a go. I spent ages on it yesterday.'

'I'd rather just play,' says Mark.

I pass the hat to Jay who sticks his hand in, pulls out a line and reads, *Think of all the hate*...then smiles. 'Can I have more of that? More hate? Gimme another line.' In he goes again – *In our dry cellar.* 'There's nothing worse than a dry cellar,' Jay laughs, 'Lots of hate, heh heh'.

'Tom,' says Mark. 'Yer nuts – you know that.'

It's a struggle, but this is what turns out:

Think of all the hate
There is in the stuffed men
Think of all the hate
In our dry cellar
Those who have crossed
Remember us not as lost
We're inbetween the motion
And the hollow men
This is the way the world ends
On the eve of destruction

'There!' I exclaim, victoriously.

'Oh god,' groans Mark, 'We just want to play songs normal-like. Your words are rubbish.'

'They can't be. They're written by two of the greatest poets in the history of stuff. PF Sloan and TS! Come on – Jay? Give it a shot. Go E on guitar. Go wang-wang on E and I'll start singing it.'

Jay cracks up, 'Wang-wang!'

'Come on man, just do anything. I'll pick up the song. *This is the way the world ends...*'

'On a D7 chord!' says Mark.

Ha ha Mark and Jay laugh.

'No...' adds Jay, '...on a D7 space shuttle called Apollo 3. Can we add that? Can you sing that in there too Tom?'

'Sing anything,' I explain, 'Change the words every time we sing the song. No one does that - change the order, change the chords, sing anything, play anything. It's like freeform.'

'I just wanna play *She's So Fine...'* mumbles Mark.

'Jay...whut about you?'

'I'd like to think about it Tom before bloody doing it,' says Jay, sticking his hand back in the hat. 'I mean, what are we supposed to do with this one? *Here we go round the prickly pear?* Heh heh. I'm picking you to pieces aren't I Tom! There's some weird stuff in that hat.'

'Look...' says Mark, '...Bob's coming down the drive. Let's git into some proper songs.'

Bob walks in. Hello Bob. Plug Mark in. 'We've got your drums set up man. You should hear what Jay got up to last night'.

'Wanna beer? I'll have anothery.'

'No thanks, not for us.'

We kick off with *Bring It On Home To Me.*

'Play *Poison Ivy...'.* Mark's calling the shots now.

('You told me this was *your* band?' Bob whispers to me.)

'Let's practice *Glad All Over.'*

Glad All Over.

'Now, *My Generation.'*

My Generation.

'Do *Slow Down.'*

Slow Down.

'How bout *You Really Got Me?'*

You Really Got Me.

'The Loved One.'

The Loved One.

'How bout *Irene?'* (My suggestion.)

'No bloody way,' says Mark. 'Not bloody *Irene.* We're a cover band. We don't do original material unless it's good stuff and there's nothing good about cut-ups and nothing good about a bloody song you wrote when you were 15!'

'Sure, but John Lennon was 15 when he wrote *Love Me Do.'*

'But you're not him.'

'I can be anything I wanna be Mark. Last week you did a big number on me about us being a *group* – yet we've just run through a whole buncha songs chosen by you. When's it gonna be my turn? I mean – while you're getting with Samantha and Jay's pissing-on with Stu, I'm sitting home trying to come up with something different!'

'Okay, okay...' says Mark. 'Jay, chuck me a beer and let's do something Tom reckons. Just not the bloody hat again – okay?'

'Okay.'

Bob just sits behind the kit, waiting, waiting. Dammit, I'm not gonna give in. I'm sure I've got Bob & Salli onside and Mr Kennedy said, 'Never, ever give up'. So here we go.

'Here's some lyrics I wrote last night...' Mark and Jay look like they might interject, but I cut them off, 'No hat - nothing like that. Okay?'

'Okay.'

'It's called *Communist Girls* and it goes:

My mother said I never should
Play with the Communist Girls in the wood
But I'm not kiddin, listen to me
Communist Girls are the girls for me.
I like left toes and I love a left hand
The right-hand side isn't half as grand
I like left toes and I'll suck a left thumb
The right-hand side isn't half the fun.

'It's great Tom,' Mark concedes, 'makes sense for a change. What's the tune?'

'Well...maybe we can make up a kinda tune that changes every time we perform it.'

'Godstruth mate. You get me so frustrated man. We doan wanna get onstage and do unrehearsed weird stuff. We're there to entertain. The audience wants songs they can dance to. We either do that or I fucken quit.'

'Listen! Wait!' I pick up a guitar and strum E over and over, 'I'll just make it up as I go along...it's – what did Samantha call that music? - *Psychedelic!* ' I add, changing to E7.

'Don't bother...' says Jay, placing his hand on the neck of my cheap Jap guitar. 'We're not putting shit on you Tom.'

I play a few disconnected chords.

'It's awful – okay?' says Jay. 'The worst tune I've ever heard.'

Mark joins in, all sincere. 'I'm not pulling an ego-trip, really I'm not. It's just that we can't play that song, cos it isn't a song. There's no bloody chord changes, no tune, it's not psychedelic, it's just a mess.' 'But the words are okay.'

'The words are fine, but it needs a riff, a jump-beat. Bob, what do you reckon?'

Don't. Don't. Don't let me down Bob – please! Bob shakes his head, 'Sorry Tom, the tune's nowhere.'

'You bastards! I wanna do original material! I want us to have our own sound! I wanna be like no other band!'

'We like the lyrics, for chrissakes. Just read the next verse...'

'Okay...

I was sent to school on the part of town
Where Communist Girls could not be found
I ran from the playground into the parks
And sat with the girls who read Karl Marx...

At which, Mark actually laughs!

I like red cheeks and a red red nose
Deep red lips and red underclothes
Red hair and freckles, listen here Mum
Darker places aren't half the fun.

'I doan know why you'd want to waste it by stuffin up the music. I'd give it a shot, cept I don't write riffs,' says Mark. 'Honest mate, I'd like to do something with it but I haven't got that kind of confidence.'

'Could you leave it with me a coupla days?' says Bob unexpectedly.

'Sure.'

*

After band practice we meet up with Clayton and we all head to a Loved Ones concert in the city. Salli meets us on the steps of the Sydney Town Hall and this time I'm not late.

Mark meets up with Samantha. She's wearing a paisley top and flowers in her hair. Bob says he's waiting for someone too, but she doesn't turn up.

'I doan know where she's got to,' says Bob. 'Maybe she's not allowed...?'

'Why not?'

'Because I'm black.'

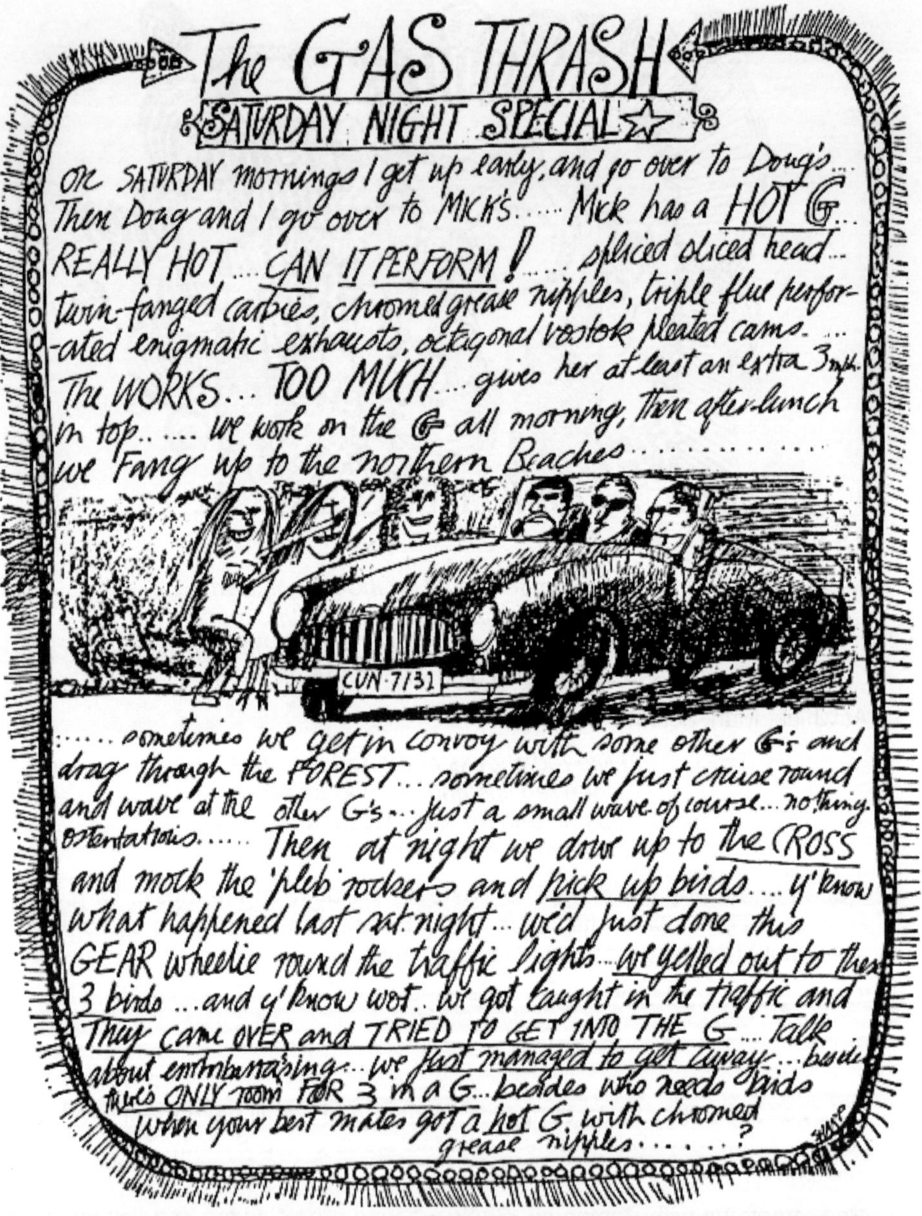

The GAS THRASH
SATURDAY NIGHT SPECIAL
On SATURDAY mornings I get up early, and go over to Doug's... Then Doug and I go over to MICK'S...... Mick has a HOT G... REALLY HOT .... CAN IT PERFORM! ...... spliced sliced head... twin-fanged carbies, chromed grease nipples, triple flue perforated enigmatic exhausts, octagonal vostok pleated cams. .... The WORKS... TOO MUCH ... gives her at least an extra 3 mph. in top...... we work on the G all morning, then after lunch we Fang up to the northern Beaches..........
CUN·7131
...... sometimes we get in convoy with some other G's and drag through the FOREST... sometimes we just cruise round and wave at the other G's... just a small wave of course... nothing ostentatious...... Then at night we drive up to the CROSS and mock the 'pleb' rockers and pick up birds ... y'know what happened last sat. night... we'd just done this GEAR wheelie round the traffic lights... we yelled out to these 3 birds ...and y'know wot.. we got caught in the traffic and They came OVER and TRIED TO GET INTO THE G... Talk about embarrassing... we just managed to get away... beside there's ONLY room FOR 3 in a G... besides who needs birds when your best mates got a hot G with chromed grease nipples......?

9

Undecided

Those harbour lights are so bloody romantic it makes you feel like throwing up. The Opera House under construction, the Rocks, those little parks tucked under the pylons...if you know Sydney you know all about those Great Big Harbour Bridge Blues and that almost-peaceful feeling you get when you're sitting under it with Bob and Salli.

The light plays with the water like skim- stones. I watch that lazy ole Manly Ferry doing its slide across this peaceful stretch of water that's actually jam-packed with sharks, so they reckon.

The Loved Ones is the greatest band in the whole world and we've just been to their concert. Gerry Humphreys is the Voice – as good as Eric Burdon of the Animals and Stevie in the Easybeats. Humphreys isn't as good-looking as Jim Keays of the Masters Apprentices, cos no one is. Girls wet themselves watching Jim. But who needs looks when you've got a fucken voice like that.

Yownder she's wawkin.
She kerms my way.
Reyd dress own.
Her lawng black hay-yer.
Tawkin lay-erk. Wawkin layk. Wantin layk.
She kerms to me...

Bring it awl back baybee, everythingweeverdidwas wrawng...

*Ahh look at yeooo with ye-or sad daryk eyes...*jumping up and down, spinning his finger, leaping, yelling, screeching to screaming girls and to me cos I went right down the front cos I've never seen anyone quite like Gerry. Tonight all I can do is talk about Gerry. Can white men sing the blues? Gerry can sing anything. Funny, I guess, a lot of girls there screamed more for Ronnie Burns than for the Loved One. But not Salli, she was on my side. Anyway she's not a screamer. *Yownder she's wawkin.* Can't believe I got so close!

Harbour lights. Luna Park winking at us, staring at the three of us with fire in its eye. If Gerry's the Voice, this is the Mouth.

'Can blue men sing the whites,' laughs Salli.

'Turn on, tune in, drop dead,' I reply, all funny-like. 'Come on Bob – git into it. What's that joke you made off a Beatles song the other day...?"

'Can't remember.'

'You know...*Drive My Car* – Baby you can drive my Volkswagon...? You did a whole routine about it. Do it again for Salli. *Baby you can drive my Merc. Yes you are a brown suit jerk...*? Come on Bob. Salli wants to hear it. It killed me.'

'Leave me alone.'

'Can't you see he's upset,' says Salli. 'Leave im alone.'

Bob walks ahead, taking a wild kick at some pebble.

'Didn't you like the Loved Ones, Bob?'

'I liked em.'

'I almost completely *plotzed*! Even better than the Yardbirds! Hey Bob, what about the bit where Gus & the Nomads came on and Gus made his entry from toppa the wall? He looks like The Beast – you know the Wrestling Beast. And what about…', she grabs my arm.

'Be your age Tom. Leave im alone.'

'He doan wanna be alone,' I brush her off, 'He's with us, aren't you Bob. Hey man, doan discriminate. We can't help being Honkies. Ha ha…'

'Shut up willya Tom!' she insists. 'That's the whole trouble'.

'Whuh?'

'Her ole man won't let Bob take her out cos he's black.'

'Like Stephanie's ole man won't let me date her cos of my hair?'

'Yeah, only he can't go to a barbershop an fix the problem.'

'Hey man!' I yell after him. 'Don't listen to racist arseholes. Come back here wiv us man!'

'No more Tom! You and me ain't the prob.'

'Why do parents do things like that Salli?' I ask, while Bob vanishes into the darkness. 'Why do our parents go – "those people ain't our *type* cos he's black, got long hair an she's a slut?" Why do parents talk like that?'

'Because they live in Turramurra,' she replies.

'They've upset Bob, dammit.'

'That happened three hours ago. Only you didn't notice.'

'Thanks for that. I'm going after im…'

'Leave im alone.'

'I'm going after im to tell him he's my mate. He needs that.'

'He *knows* that. It's not you that's bothering him. It just that Turramurrans don't like part-Aboriginals kissin their daughters. My parents wouldn't let me go out with him.'

'How do you know all this?'

'Because I talked to him. Bob's in love.'

The nightmare of love. The darling of it. The uncertainty. Not handsome. Not wealthy enough. You can never be worthy of her. She-ghost. My poem to stand in my place, cos I'm hopeless in the flesh.

A voice says *gimme a light man, hey man, gimme a light.* It's a big coat with a man inside it, sitting on the ground near a park bench.

'Too many problems for one man,' he says.

'What's your name?' I reply in a middleclass accent.

'My name is George Kefalonia,' says he. 'I have my own business one time and I have big accident. I had all my ribs broken.'

'Gee man yeah, that sounds like hard luck.'

'Before that, I woz a family man. I woz a man who was never touching another woman. I never take a drink in my life. I never take a drug in my life. Just live for my daughters and for my wife. And she fucken decided to leave me. I had a big job. I could work 24 hours a day if I want. But now I can't work.'

SALLI! Help!

'Yeah, yeah, yeah,' says George Kefalonia. No Beatles there. 'Yeah, I can do it. But first I need the formula to get up from these problems – becoz there 's too many problems for one man. And I am only one man. No hav brother. No hav sister. Too much for me. Too many problems at once. I doan know how I can go on. But I am very strong mate. You doan know how strong I am.'

He rises and walks into the circle of the shadow of the Bridge. He joins the moon.

'I am no good any more!' he cries into the teeth of Luna Park. 'Coming here to this country, I doan know why!'

'Hey George, it's okay. Hang here with us.'

'I want to see you again one day…' walking away. *Wawkin.* '…and you will see George mutch better than you see im tonight.'

George.

GEORGE.

All that's left of George in the empty bottle.

Bring it on. Come on Park-people, make-show for Salli an me on our night on the town. Salli, over here quick! Lovers feelup, hand upskirt, godstruth what are we watchin now?

'Love…' she says. 'Paper-thin love. I know everything about love dammit.'

'Love?'

'Yes Tom, somthin of which you know nuthin.'

'Salli, you got me wrong…!'

'You're just like Jay – a backseater!'

'No Salli! I'm different!'

'Different, how?'

'I believe innit. In beauty. In luv. In - *there's not enough passion in the world.* Empty and blank though you may find me, I am not empty and blank.'

She asks, 'How come you kissed me in front of your friends when you had an audience, never when we're alone?'

Damn, why'd she arsk that?

'Salli,' I tell her, under the Bridge. 'I kissed you because I needed someone to kiss. It gets like that sometimes.'

'And all those backseat jobs?'

'Salli, that's not me!' (wishing it woz). 'No…!' Because of the way I walk and talk and swear and smoke and grow my hair no one believes that the answer is NO I HAVEN'T. No one ever believes that. Godstruth I wish I was cheap. I am in my mind.

But luv?

Don't kno yet what love is except for this searing pain inside called Delia-for-a-dream, Irene-for-three-months.

'Turn-on, tune-in and drop-dead.' Why am I out of reach whenever I wanna properly be reached? Bob! Where are you in the dark?

'Nah,' he replies, moody and white-womaned.

'Bob! We can't help being whiteys!'

Salli turns to me again, 'Talk to ME white boy.'

'Talk?'

'You're shallow Tom Truscott, I've heard all your raves.'

'No! Salli no! I LUV. I love you like I love the Harbour. I love you like I love an enemy. You're my best woman-friend, but we doan need to touch right now. Can't I love this way…?'

We are the Hollow Men.
We are the stuffed men.
Head piece filled with straw.

'…godstruth, there's not enough passion in the world.'

But there's passion right there in the park.

Passion in that bottle. Passion in the racist parental attitudes against Bob. Passion in the Fugs. Passion in Sydneytown on this empty Friday night. I can smell it.

Salli speaks, 'You won't know what love is Tom until you learn to fight for it. You don't know what it's like to feel yourself turning a little mad because you've loved so much and got nothing in return. To love someone so much you really want to hurt them for all the hurt they've given you. To be always looking to a future, which gets more and more distant as you reach out to it. To twist the truth in your mind to believe you have some hope of getting it and then have everything shattered by a couple of words. Or someone else.'

'Salli? Are you calling me?'

'To love someone,' she says with iron, 'so that you know the meaning of hate'.

That's the first time all night we get Bob's attention.

Thank ke-ryst someone knows what she's talking about.

THERE'LL
BE A
BIT OF A
PARTY
TOMORROW
NIGHT
ITS VERY
GOOD TO
SEE YOU

10
Friday On My Mind

'Tom!'

No answer.

'Tom!'

'What's wrong with the boy I wonder. *You* Tom!'

I'm writing, that's whut. And when I'm writing a poem, there ain't no one can disturb me. Would they yell 'C'm ere!' in the middle of Bill Shakespeare knocking out a casual sonnet?

Let me not unto the marriage of true minds admit impediments... 'Bill, flush the toilet willya!'

I've got this great idea for a poem called *Guilt In Two Parts, A+B.* (Great title!) Goes like this: 'You only fear the guilt when the pain's not worth the fun...'. Dunno whut comes next.

'Tom!'

I'm studying in the library and I've got my tranny in my ear. Can't hear a thing except Snoopy V the bloody Red Baron in song. I think I'll write an abstract poem and blow everyone away. A very abstract poem. 'Guilt A+B' was too regular.

I'll write in a new revolutionary style, more different that Bob Dylan's *Eleven Outlined Epitaphs* and Woody Guthrie who he copied it all from.

'Tom!' There's that voice again. I unclip my earpiece, tuck the poem away and look up. Oh, it's all right. It's Calder the Ancient History teacher (and Deputy Head) who never gives me a hard time because I'm his best hope as a Level One student provided I don't get expelled before sitting the exam.

'Congratulations,' he says. 'Your essay would get a good pass even at university level'. He hands it back with a big 'A' in the top corner. Ha Devlin, suck eggs. Here's 12 good pages and Bibliography. Plus I might've also bin half-decent at English but I've got an idiot for a teacher. He likes Keats & Wordsworth. I don't like that ole stuff, cept *We'll Go No More A-Rovin,* which is in *The Catcher in the Rye.*

Tomorrow night we're having a class party. They're always boring.

Mark and Samantha reckon they're in luv. Yuk. Nowadays she's much easier to take than when we first met. She lends me a Grateful Dead LP and gives Mark heaps of new ideas.

Bob still doesn't talk. Doesn't open up. Like, 'Hey man, I've got girlfriend-father troubles'. None of that. Not Bob. He comes to band practice and grunts when we ask about his girlfriend. It was kinda awkward hearing him say 'because I'm black'. There's something frightenin about that because you doan notice until someone says 'just when you thought we were all equal…let's start picking you off, starting with the blacks, then the wogs, next the Commies and eventually we'll get to the longhairs and those who doan think right thoughts. *No one is innercent.*

I like Jay a lot. Not Stu so much. I like Jay because he's honest, tells you upfront what he thinks. And he's fun. Parents don't agree but I doan reckon he's trying to do any harm. He's a bit blue though about his dead father an he talks about how they used to go fishin together on the Hawkesbury.

I'm in the library. I just got an A for Ancient History. So I write a poem.

Mybe nobody knOws thatb a bject

feeling called despair. Maybe it's

something everyone's afraid of.

Maybe, Maybe, Maybe.

When you're all alone

Out of control/

% tired %$

I guess you gondwre wondeer qharf on eaRTH

dix i doc wrojnngf tpo deseerve thuis.

This is thecend man. This is the end.

So young. m Eso young.

young – I qa nam so young. +

Aso much ub doubt.

So much.

TROO much jun lovew.

And in treoble.

Nohbody wants me. Only you.

Poem.
By Me.

All I've got to do is set it to music an I'll have a song for the Blitz to hate.

Just as the bell goes, Kennedy walks into the library.

'Mr Kennedy! Mr Kennedy!'

'Shooossssh…' says the Librarian who always carries on about Dewey. Like a Walt Disney duck character.

'Mr Kennedy, I've just written a brilliant poem!' He comes over and I show him. 'Is this Hip or whaaat?'

'Well…er…', he scratches his beard. 'I suggest you…ah…might, try putting in slashes, so it reads:

Mybe nobody knOws/thatb a bject/feeling called despair/
Maybe it's/something everyone's afraid of/Maybe/Maybe/Maybe…

…something along those lines. But maybe Tom, it's not ah poem. Do you know what else it might be?

'Whut?'

'It might be a…ah…series of 25 pictures?'

'Huh?'

'Look at that word *wrojnngf.* You could write those letters on a big canvas and suggest a *wrojnngf* mood with…uh…your choice of colour. And this word – a GREAT word, *quarf.* Think what images you could conjure with a *quarf.*'

'Yeah!' I'm excited. Recognition at last! 'I'll show it to my English teacher then…!'

'…ah…no need for that…', says Mr Kennedy, rubbing red paint off his fingers. 'Some things in life aren't…ah…for everybody'.

It's another Friday. Tomorrow's Saturday.

There's a class party at Jenny's joint tomorrow night.

POP
MAN

11
All Tomorrow's Parties

Suburban raga, the day goes as days go by. Tonight's the night of Jenny's hopeless class party. I'm going because I like em and because they like me. Yeah we like each other even though I think they're a bunch of systemites and they tell me I've got some growing up to do. At least I don't go around like them saying 'sugar' instead of shit, 'basket' instead' of bastard and 'fff-froot loops' for fuck. Afterwards they go 'Aha, see - you can't accuse me of swearing'.

Fuck em.

Things are a bit strange at Mark's at the moment. Mark's place, a flat called Turramurra Gardens, which hasn't got any gardens, just lawn mowed as short as a high school haircut.

Mark's parents have gone to Noumea for a fortnight. The good news is they've left Mark the flat plus enough money to feed himself for 14 days. He immediately went out and spent everything. No probs. He bought the following albums: Loved Ones - *Magic Box,* Easybeats - *Easy,* Them – *Angry Young Them,* Spencer Davis Group – *The Second Album,* plus two Rolling Stone EPs, a new guitar strap and a spare set of strings.

He's now got no money, not even for cigs. He smokes our butts, which he rolls in pages torn out of a Bible. So we (mostly Samantha) have to keep him fed. That means - Stu stealing packets of rice from supermarkets, Mark cadging skool lunches from classmates and Jay, Clayton or me inviting him to our house around lunchtime on weekends.

I drop in on Jay who's growling around the place cos his Mum is with a new man called Charlie. He reckons they share the same bed, which plays on his mind. He says he caught them kissing in the kitchen. On the good side, this guy gives Jay money and cigarettes. I reckon *Kissing in the Kitchen* is a great song title.

'Not bad…' says Jay, '…rhymes with bitchin.'

This arvo we're hanging at Mark's place. Samantha drops in with a pie for Mark. Then she sits on the couch, gets Mark to sit on the carpet between her knees and brushes his hair. Me & Clayton play 500 with him, while Jay and Stu keep talking about Jay's Mum's man. When Jay flashes the money Charlie gave him, Stu snatches it immediately, 'Great, let's get a bottle of bourbon!' Everybody goes, 'Yeah!' So everyone, cept Samantha, Mark and Clayton, go hairing down to the grog shop.

Coming back Jay and Stu try to figure out how to knock off a Council sign. As an idea, it's brill. And then. And then, damn him. Stu does something mean. Just for the heck of it.

As we're walking back, we've gotta cross the sidestreet. Me and Bob skip quickly across in front of a Cortina that's making the turn. Being in a smartarse mood, Jay takes it just slowly enough to bother the driver. Now Stu's gotta go one better. He deliberately drops his lighter in the path of the Cortina and takes his time picking it up. Doesn't even look at the driver, who has one of two choices – either hit the pedestrian or jam on his brakes. He goes for the brakes. Crash. There's a car on his tail.

Then another crash, a Mini makes it a threesome. Red and orange glass everywhere. Swearing. Kid crying. And a sad-faced man hauls himself outta the driver's door, looks around and says, 'There was a teenager...!' and before anyone can say, 'grab those lads' we're back inside Mark's place.

'You deliberately caused that!' Jay accuses.

'Good huh?' laughs Stu.

'That kid might have bin hurt!'

'She wasn't.'

'You're some mean bastard Stu!'

Stu gives him the finger and wanders into the kitchen. Me and Bob doan know what to say. (Anyway, Stu hates Bob – don't know why - there's a blue right there, just waiting to happen). Clayton is genuinely freaked out. He saw it all from the upstairs verandah. Of all of us, Clayton is the most bitten by Peace & Love. He even tries to get along with his parents. And he believes the world could be a better place if we all give it our best shot. He and Stu argue.

'I don't give a *shit* about peace & love!' announces Stu.

That's what sinks Clayton. He thinks everyone believes in love, peace and god. 'It's intrinsic,' he reckons.

'What does intrinsic mean?' asks Stu, 'ya poofta'. And before there's an answer, Stu shoves Clayton outta his way and punches me in the arm, just for being in the road. Now that he's belted me, Stu seems happy again. He puts the argument aside, gathers Jay and heads for the Cross.

That leaves Mark, Samantha, Clayton, Bob and me. Cept I'm booked for my non-alcohol class party and Mark's invited too, cos he's in the same class. But Mark reckons he wants to stay with Samantha instead. Then the phone rings. Clayton picks it up. It's Salli, tracking me I s'pose. I signal to Clayton, 'I'm not here!' (because she'd hate the party and it's too complicated to re-organise a whole new thing).

'Come over here then,' Clayton tells her. 'Mark's got a heap of new LPs. Tom's gone to a class party. Yeah, bring Jayne too. Click. Clayton turns to us and says, 'Salli and Jayne'll be here in half an hour'.

'Then we might go with Tom,' says Samantha. 'I can't *stand* her. She's a cat.'

'I'll leave the key then,' Mark flicks it to Clayton, grabs a jacket and says, 'We're pissing off with Tom if that's okay. You'll be right, eh?'

'We'll get by,' Clayton nods.

So Samantha's coming and I'm not confident about introducing her to our unhip classmates. Most of them are Proddys or Tykes. Man, they're not even hip to Cream and certainly not ready for the Dead.

'I'll bring the plonk...' Mark tucks the bourbon inside his jacket and off we go. Bob tags along too.

'No probs.'

'Bout time you fessed up to us about your girlfriend?' says Samantha, going straight for the sore point with Bob.

I can't understand why everyone suddenly wants to crash Jenny's party. I was only going cos I promised Janet I'd be there. While waiting for the train it all comes clear. It's the food supplies. Mark explains that they'll hide near the back fence – somewhere like that – while I keep going in-and-out with pockets of food for Mark to take home. We can grab the food and maybe come back to his flat. Then the train comes. We get in the back carriage and pass the bourbon around.

I arrive at Jenny's way after the rest of the class, leaving Bob, Samantha and Mark behind the back fence as agreed. Mark tells me a zillion times to get heaps of biscuits cos they don't squash up in pockets and to go easy on the cheese. Oh yeah, and *meat.* Meat is good. My excuse – he says – for going outside all the time is that I've gotta have a smoke.

*

Knock knock. It's me Jenn. Hello and stuff. Mmm, luv yer new party dress. Jenny comes laughing alongside me and tells me I missed the trick they pulled on Heather whose b'day it is and I forgot that was the whole point of the party and forgot to bring a bloody prez.

Apparently Heather told Jenny that her Mum bought her a new bra and pants set. 'Gis a look,' Jenny said, with all the class hiding under the settee, behind curtains, etc. And Heather lifted her frock and out leapt all the lads happy birthdaying and yelling *ha ha saw yer pance!*

'What colour?' is what interests me.

'Baby blue,' says Jenny, 'with frilly bits'. Whooah! Sorry I missed the frillies! Heather peeps me out across the room with an aw shucks look. God, it's amazing why girls play along with this I'm-so-embarrassed shit when you know they're really damn well not.

'Sorry I forgot to buy you a prezzie Heather', kissing her happy birthday hello. She doesn't mind, knowin I'm the kinda guy who forgets everything including the anniversary of nailing Jesus and the Anzacs.

'Did you bring your guitar Tom?' asks John Vote Pye.

'Nah mate.'

'Such a pity you didn't bring it,' says Jenny, who is above all things nice.

'What did the sheep say to the shearer?' says Colin Prefect Ransome.

'Dunno.'

'Eu-calyp-tus...' long pause, then, 'you know - *yeu-clipped-us!*' Ha ha ha. Everyone ha ha hars, including me. Not cos it's funny but cos it's polite.

'Here's a good un,' I sing out. 'The Pope turns up in Sydney, gets off the plane, the ticket collector says: *Welcome to Australia Mr Presley.* He goes, *I'm not Mr Presley.* Goes to the cab rank, sez *Take me to the hotel where the Beatles stayed.* Cab driver sez, *Anything you say Mr Presley.* The Pope goes, *I'm not Mr Presley.* Gets to his hotel room and a beaoootiful hooker in black underwear says, *Mr Presley, I'm here to take care of your every need.* Pope snaps his fingers and goes, *One for the money!*

No one laughs. Must be more Tykes here than I thought. I try again, '*One fer the murney, two fer the show...*'. Still nothing.' Okay, here's anothery – there's a girl at the station, bra all ripped and torn...'. Jenny's mum arrives next to me in time for the punchline, '...I've bin graped - there was a whole bunch of em!'

'Oh well,' says Mrs Jenny, 'I suppose it could have been a whole lot worse'. Yeah Mrs Mother, it certainly coulda bin a whole lot worse. You should cop Stu's period joke. Bob slips in the back door and sidles up.

'Hey man, I thought you were in hiding?'

'Yeah, but I got bored.'

'Hello Bob,' Jenny welcomes him. 'We didn't expect you here...' (of course she didn't, he's in a younger class) '...but you're certainly welcome'.

'Thanks for having me,' he replies, slipping a couple of party franks into his coat pocket for Mark's sake amen.

'Bob! Hello!' This is Adrian School Captain Sport Hero. Big manly handshake, 'Good to see you ole son! Come to play us a song, ha ha har!'

'I've got a nylon-string guitar in my room,' Jenny says, and I follow her down the hall into this pink bedroom with teddy bears, dolls, floral curtains, fluffy carpet and Jane Austen assignments lying around.

I carry out the guitar and Jenny pulls the party up and announces, 'Bob and Tom are going to sing a duo'. Everyone pays attention. I look at Bob, he takes the guitar and says, 'I'll play – you sing'. Oh, what the heck. We do *Don't Think Twice, It's All Right* and *Masters of War.* The class claps politely. We don't know whether they liked it or not because they're the sorta people who clap to be nice. Next Jenny pulls out the sheet music to *The Sound of Silence* which Bob strums and she sings, and we don't mind cos we're here to please while stealing sausage rolls and frankfurts. Oh no, they move to *Yesterday*. Then, everyone sings *All My Trials* and they leave us alone. She puts the *Sound of Music* on the turntable. *Edelweiss – Idle Vice,* ha ha.

'Hey man,' says Bob. 'Check this out...' he pulls off a riff.

'Like it? It's for *Communist Girls*.'

'Again?'

Bob plays the riff off the fifth fret and sings in a whisper, 'My mother said I never should…' – riff. '…play with the Communist girls in the wood…' – riff.

'It fits! Do yer reckon Mark & Jay'll like it?'

'Does that matter?'

'Huh?'

'I didn't write it for them, writing it was jess somethin to do.'

Then Jenny's Mum crosses the room, saying 'lovely' this and 'lovely' that, to whatever shit my classmates are saying. She spots Bob and offers her hand like the Lady Duckmanton. 'How lovely to see you here Bob. How very *spontaneous* of you. And thank you and Tom for playing those tunes.'

'Sure,' shrugs Bob, fiddling with his hendrix while Jenny's Mum tells him to help himself to nibblies which, judging by the bulge in his pockets, he already has. Time to unload, I think.

'I er think I might just duck outside,' I tell Jenny and her Mum.

'Not taking a furlough already?' says Mrs Jenny.

'Huh? Er no – just popping out for a cig…'

'Surely you don't *smoke* Tom?'

'Just a bit.' O god.

'It's okay if Tom smokes inside Mum, isn't it?'

'Certainly Jenny,' she answers. 'I was simply questioning the deleterious affect on his lung capacity?'

'Then I'll get an ash tray.'

'No, no – don't worry about it Jenn. I'll just stand on the back porch…' and before anyone can argue, I open the French doors, walk past the pool and hear Bob going *pssst! Pssst!*

Mark answers with his owl hoot, which sounds nothing like any birdlife. Me and Bob locate Mark and Samantha, empty out our pockets and get sent back for more.

'Whaddaya mean MORE!'

'You trying to starve me? Swig this…' he passes the bourbon. 'Bob?'

'Not for me thanks.'

'Okay Tom, inya go.'

'Yes, in you go,' adds Samantha, which needles me.

'Shut up,' Mark tells her.

'Don't tell me to shut up.'

Bob looks at me. I look at him. First time we've heard those two take a peck at each other.

'Go on…' says Mark, passing the bottle again, 'get more party franks'. So back inside I go, without Bob this time.

Janet comes up and sits beside me. Says hi, she's pleased I got decent grades in Ancient History and Art and how am I, and all that. I go yeah pretty good thanks, nice to see ya.

Janet says I shouldn't smoke because I'll regret it later. And what do I want out of life anyway? No point in firing back the same question, I can tell by her pleated skirt and flick-up hair. Awkwardly muttering whatever, I slip my hand inside my coat and what's this? A bottle! While Janet talks about careers I pour a little bourbon into my drink and after a sip I'm surprised that it seems to be taking a small grip.

Suddenly I am enjoyin myself a bit more. Loosenin up. Giving em my best shot. Not going ahh what a boring party folks. Getting more and more into it. How about a bit of a strum? I reach for the geetar and start banging out *My Generation.* F-f-f-fade away. They all keep talking, cept Janet, so I do *Satisfaction* so loud and fast that I am impossible to ignore. I break a string and give up.

Remembering my mission, I go back to filling my pockets with cheesecake, frankfurts, caviar, sandwiches, twisties and sliced meat. Then – reckoning I need another smoke – I head back out.

Inside I overhear someone shouting they oughta play Spin-the-Bottle, a game where you spin it then kiss the person the bottle points to when it stops. If I'd stayed inside, I might've got to kiss Janice. Good lips. I can hear Peter, Paul & Mary now and through the curtains I think I see a couple dancing a bit. How can you dance to P/P/&M? I think that might be John kissing Heather. That's Adrian pashing Janice fer sure.

I squat in the long grass with Mark and Samantha and realise the weather's turned up drizzle. Samantha's got an umbrella only big enough for two, so Bob and me are being rained on. I dig out the food and pass the bottle to Bob, 'spin the bottle inside, pass the bottle out here!'

'Okay…' and he takes a swig. And we talk. I reckon the people inside aren't as groovy as us, they aren't as *aware,* etc. We spin-out on memories of how one of us said or wore somethin that really turned suburban heads. But no one is pleased with what Stu did. No one does that. No one mentions Stu calling the Milk Bar guy a wog.

Samantha keeps coming up with new ideas for the band. She reckons we should cover Scott Mackenzie's *When you're going to San Francisco, be sure to wear some flowers in your hair…*and Mark says okay he wouldn't mind singing it - cos I won't. Samantha also reckons I should grow a beard. I reply that I'm a Mod and wouldn't be caught dead in bloody whiskers. Then clothes. She says we oughta wear kaftans and paisley. Ferget military disposal gear. That's all old hat, she says.

'I simply don't like American stuff,' I tell her. 'I like Carnaby Street and Euro stuff'.

'But you're a bit of a bitzer aren't you? How'd you get a handle like Truscott?'

'A bitzer maybe, but not a wog.'

'Oh no,' all agree, 'not a wog'.

'Where's that bottle?'

I doan wanna be a hippie, I tell Samantha. I like my hair long as attitude - not as a mess like them. I like good clothes and Beatle boots. I hate Indian gurus and Kombis. Doan wanna be the next new thing. Doan wanna turn the page and keep turning. I wanna find something right and stick with it. And, this is it. I'm speaking now from the heart, but is she listenin? Inside of answering, she says – frankly – that Mark is easily the best-looking guy in our band ('no offence Bob and Tom…') and should therefore be the singer not me.

Terrific. Just what I need to hear.

'What do you think Bob?' she says, doing that cutsey eye-flutter routine.

'Oh,' he replies, 'I reckon we should pro'bly have a go at *Communist Girls* next practice, if it's okay with Mark?'

'Yeah,' says Mark. 'Sure. If the tune works, let's give it a go. Go get me more food guys…' he points, '…this rain can't be much fun'.

'Do it yerself,' says Bob, 'I'll wait for youse down the shops'.

'Yeah Tom, you go…'

My head's spinning a bit. I feel a touch spewy but I'm also beginning to feel terrific at the same time. I walk off for a pee. Bob joins me before heading off. I whack my arm around his shoulders.

'Hey man, I've never told you this before but all this girlfriend shit you're going through – you oughta talk about it. I doan even know her name?'

'Louise.'

'Loo-eeze. Is she nice?'

'Korse she's nice.'

'Blonde? Brunette? Or whut?'

'Hey you guys!' That's Adrian. 'Whut are you stupid baskets doing in the rain?'

'They're soaked,' adds Heather.

'A whole lot of soakin goin on!' I reply, thinking I'm being funny. 'Fuck off Adrian. I've bin wanting to tell Bob this stuff for ages. There's whiteys and honkys. Some are okay but oldies oughtta be shot at 30. Know what I mean bout whiteys and shiteys…?'

'Yeah.'

'Know what I mean about people who ain't Rock n Roll and doan understand nuthin man? And then there's guys like Jay – I mean, he's a great guy. A bloody GRATE guy. So's Mark. Mark's a bloody GRATE guy too. Know what I mean?' I say, hugging him a bit.

'Yeah.'

'Just like you're a GRATE guy Bob. We're mates – right?'

'Yeah.'

'Tom! Get inside!' That's Adrian again.

'I am inside!'

'You're not!'

'I'm inside a shed!'

'You're SOAKED!'

I remove my arm from Bob's shoulder and we walk inside. I don't stop talkin, 'I couldn't tell you this before Bob, but honest – look around at my classmates. I mean, they're all deadshits but they're also GOOD PEOPLE…' Janet's staring at me, wondering what I might come out with next. 'I really MEAN UT! Jenny's ole dear is nice. Adrian's fucken bossy. Daks is fucken nuts. Colin's fucken straight. But they're all okay. Know what I mean?'

'Yeah,' says Bob, 'I know what you mean'.

'An sorry I said that thing about whiteys, but just because…' I take another swig, '…an jess becoz Louise's ole man doesn't want you around – well, not everyone wants me or Jay around huh? Nor Clayton. An nobody wants Stu!'

Suddenly I feel like a real idiot for coming back inside. Adrian says I've been impolite but I doan kno why cos I reckon I'm being honest fer a change. Ian sez my clothes are all wet. I tell him that's god's fault cos he made it rain. Colin sez that's 'blasphemous' and I say nothing's blasphemous cos blasphemy is treatin religin like any uvver subjeck. Bleah.

Jenny races over, 'I've got him, it's all right.'

'Wheer's Bob?' I arsk.

'Changin his shirt, and you should too…'

'Where iz he? I'm in the middle of explainin somethink impotent…!'

Colin asks what's going on? I go huh. He arsks why I'm wet and wants to know why I'm tryin to stuff a lamington into my pocket.

I knock over a jug of lemonade, which is empty, but still goes crash. Then Janet takes my arm and sits me down. I try to make a joke. *The Pope turns up at the airport…*and then I laugh a bit longer than I should've which embarrasses me because there's something scary about being the last one left laughing. Especially when it's a long laugh and allofasudden you realise that you were not just the first but the only laugher.

So I sit with Janet and tell her all about the band and *Communist Girls* and that Samantha says we should switch from being Mods to Hippies and that I like some of her ideas but not all. I tell Janet that nobody in the Blitz appreciates my ideas cept Bob and that Bob's a GRATE PERSON and she is too. I tell her the main thing in life is to love each other and live a peaceful life playing loud Rock music and painting. I take a swig from the bottle and Adrian grips my shoulder and says, 'I think you've had enuff for the present'. He tries to grab the bottle.

I won't hand it over. Instead I go, 'Okay, see if I care...' and put it on the hall table and knock over a china thing.

Jenny returns with a strong coffee and sez, 'drink this' and as soon as Adrian returns to Janice, I pour another nip.

'Merci pour le lamington...' I say to Jenny's ole dear walking past, trying to talk high school French to charm her. 'C'est la guerre pussycat...ha ha...and l'amour as in la mer?'

She replies with a sentence with the word *gâteau* in it that I just don't understand but I answer with something about the Great Gatsby – *gateau/Gatesby* - but realise I didn't actually say anything at all. Then I put my hand in my pocket and it comes out covered with cream and little black caviar balls. I don't feel like laughing. Something I thought extremely funny 30 seconds ago is now extremely sad. I wipe my hand on my jeans.

Janet wants to know what I plan to do with my future. I tell her we can do anything we want because we're all part of God-Buddha-Jesus-Krishna. Plus I've been reading the *Tibetan Book of the Dead*.

Janet tells me the Lord Jesus Christ is the Lamb of God who died for my sins on Calvary, and a Roman soldier shoved this huge great big spear in his side, which ran blood and water because of what I do wrong. The Lord God Jesus Christ would forgive all my sins if I asked him to. So I pray God to forgive catching the train without a ticket, saying fuck and feeling Karen's tits. I also confess to heroin addiction, sodomy, pack-rape, murder, incest and arson. When I see the expression on Janet's face I unexpectedly break into sobs.

I keep hearing the occasional 'how's Tom?' plus people keep patting me. Janet's got her arm around my shoulder and I'm babbling something about the Sheep of God and the Koala of God. I want to leap up and say, 'I'm fine' but I can't.

Jenny picks up my coffee, sniffs it, takes it away and returns with another one. Somewhere I can hear Simon and Garfunkel on the turntable. Next thing I know Samantha is caressing my forehead ('Samantha! What are *you* doing here?') Janet is holding my hand.

'Time to go, mate,' says Bob.

'Wha..? Nah, it's ah...'.

'He's a bit depressed I think,' explains Janet.

'I'll just pick up my geetar an go...'.

'You didn't bring one.'

'What wuz I playin then? Did I bring a coat? Where is it?'

'You're wearing it.'

'Oh.'

'C'mon Tom.'

'One more thing…'.

'What's that?'

'Janet…?'

'Tom.'

'Janet, believe me when I say – there's not enuff…ah…passion in the world.'

'Right.'

'Wuz that good?'

'Yeah Tom, it was good.'

'Wuz that percivtiv…aer…I mean, perceptive?'

'Yes, very.'

'And one more thing Janet. We doan wanna make a fuss. I'll just slip out the back. I doan want anyone to know about this…'.

'Goodbye Tom,' says Jenny, and everyone's heads turn as I leave. 'Thanks for coming'. I walk outside and suddenly realise it's not as late as I thought.

'Janet, can I kiss you goodnight?'

She says no, 'go home to bed'.

'Where's Mark?'

'At Ashfield Station,' Samantha replies, tugging me in the opposite direction.

The three of us walk to the station – Samantha, Bob and me. Somewhere along the way I take a pee in someone's rose garden. I also spew there. And when I do, I suddenly start to feel great again.

Mark is waiting for us at the bus stop opposite nearby. We find him, no probs.

'Did ya grab any more food?'

'Yes I did,' I put my hand in my pocket and pull out three mashed cheesy sandwiches, a lamington and an empty bourbon hip flask.

'Jeez mate,' he shakes his head, 'I hope it wuz all worth it'. He looks at this mash and chucks it straight into a rubbish bin. Says, 'C'mon back to my place, shower, straight'n up an I'll play you my new records'.

That's what it's all about, I guess.

12

Desolation Row

I saw the best minds of my generation destroyed by maths and science,
mowinglawnseverySunday and shiningthechrome bits on their cars;
Drugging themselves with the Ed Sullivan Show and Engelbert
Humperdink with never a good word for the Grateful Dead;
Never asking the obvious questions like
why are we taught to respect Menzies?

Never asking why did Stevie Winwood *really* leave the Spencer Davis
Group to form Traffic;
Never asking why Frank & Nancy Sinatra are top of the pops with
something stupid;
Never asking, who is the real passenger in the Beatles?
Never asking why Dad, like every other Dad, hates marijuana but
spends every Friday night at the Greengate getting blind;
Never asking why Jimi Hendrix was the support act for the Monkees?

Stop the hoax.

Never asking about Lennie Bruce, cos we don't know who he is,
but we know about Keats;
Never asking anything about Woody Guthrie;
Never asking – when said about a longhair – 'is it a boy or a girl?' is
considered cutthroat wit in this suburb;
Never asking why parents who don't believe in god think that we should
all attend the local St Andrews Church;

Never asking why Allen Ginsberg's howl is all we need to know about
poetry. For godsakes hold your tongue and let me love. Love lie with
me. Lie down with me. Without you they'd forget to change the weather.
I want you *soooo* bad. I love you like I love an enemy. Cut my thoughts.
With your sad dark eyes.

I saw the best minds of my generation watching the *Man from UNCLE.*
I heard the best voices of my generation viet-namming against their
parents and shrieking mindless empty protests from the heart never
knowing why or why not.

I heard every nuisance kid in town arguing with frightened parents about drugs. The Dept of Health sent around brochures of a before/after drugs person slowly disintegrating and parents saying of the last photo of the degraded person, 'that could be you on drugs'.

And every parent panicked. Ransacked bedrooms. Intercepting backpockets of jeans on their way to the wash. Checking arms while we're asleep. Lifting mattresses and muttering to themselves, 'it's got to be stashed *somewhere*' but mostly it wasn't.

Hanging around Kings Cross is lame in skool uniform. I walk into the *Head Shop.* I ask her - hippie dress and beads behind the counter - if she can sell me some 'grass'? Yeah, grass. You know.

Scratches her head. 'I'm cool – you know, *grass'* - mary jane, gunja, mull, reefer, herb superb, hootch, dope, green, weed, keif, smoke, tea, pot – *marry-didge-uarna*?'

A shoulder-length hair guy flashes through the beaded backroom curtains. Looks worried til he spots the uniform – case n all. Smiles at her, 'Nope'. All over. Sorry everyone. Couldn't pull it off. Feel a bit of a jerk actually.

*

Gotta get something right. One of my better ideas is to go see Dobell who lives beyond Gosford. In the FJ on the road to his place in Wangi, we're arguing about who's best – Clapton or Hendrix?

Me: *Sunshine of Your Love*. Tops.

Jay: No Hendrix is the one. Clapton plays like his second cousin.

Me: Yeah, but Hendrix doesn't play down-the-line Blues licks.

Jay: Oh yes he does.

Me: Hendrix plays Rock N Roll.

Jay: Naah, Blues – hard on.

Me: But he's so showy.

Jay: That's different. When he plays a solo you can really hear his Blues lines, even all that cosmic stuff. Tripped-out guitar solos, washing sounds in the background of the mixes. Shimmering guitars. Cos that's where he's the Master.

Me: I thought Clapton was more like Classical Blues cos he did his time in John Mayall's Bluesbreakers.

Jay: Clapton's lots of things. In *Fresh Cream* he's like Pete Townshend in some ways. Stuff like *So Glad* – you know?

And so on.

The car plugs along the Pacific Highway, past the Henry Kendall memorial, further and further north until I yelp, 'Wangi! That's where he lives!'

Jay: Where the fuck's Wangi.

Me: At Wangi.

Clayton: Past Bateau Bay. Keep drivin.

I saw the best minds of my generation – me, Salli, Mark, Samantha, Jay, Bob and Clayton, crammed into a grey FJ Holden with red seats, heading past the Ourimbah turnoff to visit Sir William Dobell and thinking *Lucky bastard him, having us for an afternoon.*

‘Who is he?’ asks Samantha

‘A famous artist,’ I reply. ‘Kennedy told me he lives in a street named after him, so it’s gotta be Dobell Avenue, Road, Place or Crescent.

‘What’s a Dobell and a Wangi for chrissakes?’

‘Ferget it Samantha,’ says Mark, ‘he paints a bit’.

‘I met a famous artist called Robert Crumb in San Francisco…’

Well this is the guy who won the Archibald Prize and thankfully she doesn’t ask, ‘What’s an Archibald?’

It must be close because it’s on Lake Macquarie. Yay, Wangi Wangi! Just like wagga is Wagga Wagga. And Tilba is Tilba Tilba.

‘Stop dammit! That’s his road!’

‘It’s Dobell PLACE!’

‘Back up!’

‘Then whut?’

‘I’ll handle it,’ I tell them, ‘Turn round for chrissakes!’

It’s a short street. Coupla houses. Leave it to me and Clayton, we’ll get us inside.

There’s a little white railing fence around the block, not mad splattered paint stuff. Nothing to show it’s the home of a famous artist. Lemme in Wangi Boy. ‘Me & Clayton’ll handle it, stay in the car youse lot’. Knock knock.

Knock knock.

Shit, the door opens. It’s a woman inna floral dress. And one of us has to say hello, we wanna see Dobell.

‘Can I help you?’

‘Yeah, we wanna see…er…meet Sir Dobell. Kennedy is my Art Teacher…he said…!’

Slowly the door closes in our faces. Not a word. Not even ‘piss off your hair’s too long’. Just a slow-closing door and a long walk back to the car, then having to admit I couldn’t pull it off. Feel like a bit of a jerk really.

The door is suddenly pulled open. ‘Morriss?’ says a man’s voice.

It’s him!

I recognize Dobell from a newspaper picture. Wow, even if he chucks us out now we’ve actually spoken to him a bit. At least I will have, when I answer the question.

‘Yeah, Morriss Kennedy’s my Art teacher.’

He sees two of us to start with, and says, ‘Okay, come in’. Then the rest of us start pouring outta the car and he seems okay with that.

The woman is nowhere in sight and he guides us up a staircase, pausing to point out a picture of a ship, 'This is a picture my father painted'. He's really proud of this one and we'll agree with anything. Just show us how famous you are and tell us something we can boast about in Sydney when we tell em we really met you, Mr Dobell. So we go – god, the ship, wow!

Into his upstairs studio, paint strewn. Paint on the floor. Stepinit paint. Mindthepaint paint. Me and Clayton talk to him. Mark and Samantha aren't really giving much of a damn. Jay isn't Arting. Salli's going 'you pulled this one off Tom!' Bob is going yeah. Me and Clayton are going, 'surrealism, picasso, salvadore dalí, rahht on'.

Dobell explains how he mixes lacquer with paint to get that shimmer on the on the water in the Opera House picture.

Moving on to the New Guinea painting, 'The New Guinea Gallery has been waiting nine years for this one…' and he doan give a damn.

'Can I use your dunny?' says Jay. Dobell points, he goes. When Jay returns he says – there's this incredible door with a butterfly, a gumnut thing on it and a note, WOW!

'I wanna be a Rock poster artist when I leave skool,' I tell Dobell.

It takes a bit to explain that nowadays Rock Art is LP covers - like *Disraeli Gears.* How can I explain this? I try. Clayton backs me up. Dobell says yes a couple of times and moves on. *Admit me as an artist for chissakes!*

In fact the subject of Rock Art kinda switches him off. He suddenly gets interested in Bob who – godnose why – he thinks comes from New Guinea and Dobell starts rabbitting on about places and towns (like Rabaul) that he thinks Bob might know and Bob can't seem to straighten him out with a no.

'Bob's a songwriter,' I tell Dobell. I like boasting about my friends. 'We're a band.'

'Oh yes,' he smiles, that's all.

Comes a point when Dobell says, 'you'll have to go now'. So it's back down the stairs. Wow to his father's painting. Wow to the bathroom door. Bye to the woman who shut the door in our face. Regards to Kennedy, okay? No wuz. Thanks Mr Dobell. See you, Mr Dobell. See you ole man who doan know what a Rock poster artist is.

*

We leave Wangi around 4.30 and head straight to Stu's in the Cross. Who's got the petrol money? How bout a burger at Peats Ridge? Dobell this. Dobell that. Let's hurry and tell Stu. Tell everyone we met Dobell.

This is gonna kill Kennedy when I see him Monday. So yeah, we drive through the suburbs. We bag out Duff Street, Turramurra Gardens, Dumaresq Street on the way through. Boys hit town. Going to the Cross man like we're hardcore cos we've got a friend who *lives* there.

Stu lives in a Farrell Street flophouse. Shared shower, shared dunnies, he even shares his room with the next random person of the same sex who checks in. No kitchens. You cook in your own room. Electric frypan city. Everyone's got one and as we wander through we can smell that yuk smell of fried banana bread through some ole door, fried fish fingers three down, stale piss from the john.

Everything smells bad, but it all sounds good – Mingus from this room, *Rhapsody in Blue* from that. On the whole more oop-boop-ee-doo than doo-wah-diddy-diddy. A man shuffling down the hall in singlet and stubbies. A woman wearing a man's dressing gown. Every face what we from the burbs call 'characters'. Hey bop blues and scraggy women, heavy gaze over no time. Old face with a new story. Young face with a big hurt. No one fits. Everything stinks. All so exciting.

All these flophouse people – where's Mum, Dad, wife, husband, son or daughter? Where's everybody when you're all alone in a shared room, waitin for the next person to stay a fortnight? Do they steal your shirts and records when they leave?

Last time I went to Stu's some ole guy bagged me out. Swear to god I had groovier hair than him, trendier clothes, but he didn't care. Said, you'll never be hip boy. Eighteen-year olds from Turramurra who fidget cain't ever be angel-headed hipsters. So I said, tell me YOUR story?

The new guy in Stu's room is a snow-haired faggot ballet dancer. We don't call faggots 'pooftas' like our Dad's do. We call them 'micks' (as in Mick Jaggers).

'This one's a bit of a mick,' says Stu introducing his new roommate. The name's Quince, a weepy drunk who every now and then dances pirouettes so we know he's not making it up about the ballet.

Quince yabbers on while drinking dry red, not offering us any cos the wine's his and we're Stu's. Still wants to be friends though. Tawks. But the more he talks the more he weeps. It's his father he says. His ole man's big and meaty and can hit hard. He's seen his ole dear hit.

Quince fought back once and got decked trying. Shows us the scar on his chin. You've got to look pretty close to find it, but it's there all right. Definitely a scar. Quince says it's not just his ole man – sob sob – but also getting caught stealin and getting expelled from skool.

Then, not cuttin it at ballet skool. Now he can't get a job cos you can see right off that everything'd be too heavy for this skinny ballerina to lift. He can't get a clerical job cos he's dyslexic. Life's so hard he says. He can't even make it with girls, so he tried boys and now his boyfriend's dropped him.

Mark's beautiful, he says, putting a shine into his downbeat talk. Then it's back to his father hitting him with a leather shaving strap and nowadays he quite likes leather shaving straps. Something to do with leather shaving straps is why his boyfriend hiked off. Wish I could squeeze somethin in about Dobell.

Every tale is let's-cry-about-it meaningful.

Plus he goes into lots of little details, like his mum wasn't just hit, she was hit on the left cheek when she was washing a Cornish Blue teacup. And his Dad wasn't just tall, he was six feet two and his name is Alex John Charles Watterson, known as 'John'. And Quince's did six and a half years of violin lessons, loves reading the poetry of Housman and starts reciting *The Inchcape Rock*, even though even I know that wasn't written by Housman.

Everyone's wondering why we aren't listening to free poetry at the Wayside Chapel or raging at Whisky-A-Go-Go. Quince is talkin and talkin and no one can squeeze in a joke, cept maybe Stu who is drinking bourbon.

Salli is bored and going home. Bob is too, so he's hitting the trail. Clayton says he'll drive them. Mark and Samantha are pashing on and probably never heard a word.

'Aussies hate the ballet', says Quince, wincing. 'Philistines! A well-balanced Aussie has chip on both shoulders!' Oh-oh, it's pirouette-time again.

This time he doesn't quite pull it off. Sooner or later we figured he wouldn't. They were getting progressively worse. He falls like a broken marionette. Stu picks him up, props him against the wall and says *take it easy man.*

Meanwhile, Woody Guthrie's *If you ain't got the Do Re Mi…*is playing in the next room and I can hear someone laughin in Farrell Street below. 'Mummy mummy!' cries some little girl. 'Mummy mummy, he said *fuckenbloody!'* There's a world of music, drifters and grifters out there all with a damn sight better stories than Quince, I betcha. I too am beginning to want out.

What about Woody Guthrie next door? *This land is your land, this land is…*sure, I know Woody's work. I can play some. So I ask Stu who's in the next room and he says a coupla hippies. Oh? I'll go introduce myself and leave. No loss, says Stu who thinks I'm a real dweebie.

Knock knock. Hey-peace-and-love-lemme-in-I-dig-Woody-too. The door don't open. Knock knock knock. C'mon, gimme some neck and I'll play you a coupla folk tunes. Knock knock. No goddamn answer.

Suddenly I hear the sound of breaking glass from inside Stu's room. *Yelp!* Pain. Furniture bang, stumbling, falling. Stu's voice, *What the fuck!* Then *hurry! Get help!*

I hear Quince saying *Lord let me die in beauty…*

Fling-back the door. Open to blood. 'Goddamn, what's Quince done?'

'Slit his wrists!'

'Call the cops!' I scream.

'You cracked! Call a fucken *cab!* Gimme that towel.'

Quince has done it all right. 'Done it *again,'* corrects Stu. 'Doan just stand there!'

Samantha and me race into William Street. 'Cab! Cab!' Stu and Mark ease Quince along, bleeding heaps.

'Lemme see his wrists!'

'Goddamn, this isn't a bloody sideshow. Open the fucken door. I'm taking him to St Vincents. Don't come.'

Tearaway cab. Flatten it.

*

What now? After standing around going struth, shit and hell, I wanna go back to Mark and Samantha but they probably won't want me. So I go for a walk through the Cross. Need a walk.

'I'll just leave youse guys and go to the Crest or maybe the Fountain – see the Birdman of Kings Cross with his million budgies. Or I'll check out Roey Norton's goatfuck witch Art at the Kashmir or wherever Stu said it was. Or maybe walk past Sandra Nelson's strip club. Or check out bikers outside the Pink Pussycat. Or visit the Wayside Chapel and watch Webster arguing with Rev Ted. Or peer into a tatt shop. Or see a band.'

So yeah - down Victoria Road and into the Kings Cross Newsagency for cigarettes and the *Kings Cross Whisper.* I ask about the latest *OZ* but it's sold out. Pip Proud walks in and buys something.

Wow, he's a real poet. You can tell by his hair. Next stop the Wayside Disco, but what's the point in going without a date? I walk towards the Wayside Chapel wondering if I can spot someone I know or know of.

I run into Paula the Mauler who I knew from second form, and just as I think hmm, she's not as bad looking as I used to think, she starts telling me about god. Not Christ or Buddha but some ugly called His Divine Grace AC Bhaktivedanta Swami Prabhupada whose message to the world is find your mantra. I tell her my current mantra is *A Whiter Shade of Pale* and me and my band are working on *Communist Girls*. I'm off. See ya Paula.

I duck down an alleyway looking for a new friend. Pee against a wall, wondering how the Stones made international headlines for doing exactly this. Stop the hoax.

I drop into a sleazy folk club, the Ball Pants. No cover charge so I walk in and park myself against the back wall, next to a coupla drunks. An Aboriginal guy is singing straight-up-and-down Country-Johnny Cash stuff. Finishes the song, then says, 'Ladies and genitals…'.

Everybody laughs and chucks a few coins. Someone picks one up from the floor and throws it onto the stage. 'S'all right mate…too tight to throw your own!' Laughs. Then, 'This is the *House of the Rising Sun'* - Am-C-D-F-Am-C-E7. I'm getting bored man. It's maybe time to head off.

Rising Sun finishes. Then more Country. 'Here's one for Jimmy Little!' *Royal Telephone.*

*

Shuffling near the back wall. A blonde trying to get through. Melting ice cream in one hand, dead flowers in the other. When she drops them someone picks them up. 'Wear em in your hair!' Ha ha ha goes someone else. But she doan notice. S'cuse, she goes s'cuse. *You can talk to Jesus on the Royal Telephone.* S'cuse bump shove s'cuse.

When she ice creams a woman's sleeve she gets shaken and sworn at, but she doan seem to notice. Goes huh and keeps walkin towards me. I'm leavin. I'm going back to Stu's. *S'cuse me.* We rub bodies opposite ways – her going in, me going out. I'm back on the street. Must be hot dog time.

'Wanna go?' some brunette in a red dress asks.

'Pardon?'

'I said, *do you wanna go?'*

'Go where…?' The penny drops,'…oh, I see!' I hurry away. *That was actually a pro asking if I wanted to…holy shit!* Can't wait to tell Clayton and Bob. If I'd said yes I could be back in this same spot within 15 minutes having DUNNIT! Goddamn.

When I snap out of it, I spot the blonde from the Ball Pants crossing Darlinghurst Road.

She's not looking where she's going. *S'cuse me* she tells the cars. And a DS Citroen slams on the brakes. She slips, picks herself up, but instead of getting off the road she must pick up all her flowers. First Stu, now this! 'Get off the road!' I insist. There's honking and get-off-the-road stuff going on.

She must have her flowers. And she's still carryin the ice cream, which is melting like slow moving lava down her fingers. Then back on the pavement at last.

'You okay?' I hand her a little flower that she missed.

'Huh?'

'I said, *are you okay?'* We're at the El Alamein Fountain, the Birdman's there with his budgies. I take her elbow and tell her to take a breather.

'I'm with a um, can't…' her head droops forward, she says uh.

'Are you ON something?'

'Um flares.'

'Flares?'

'No – flairs, FLAIRS…'.

'Oh, flowers?'

'Yeah, the flairs were given me by a uh, ole geezer called dunno.'

'You're not safe, I'd like to help.'

'He says uh Shaynie you're none of it Shayn.'

'Shane?'

'Yep.'

'Hello Shane, I'm Tom. Call me Roger Ramjet if you like.'

'Ramjet?'

'No, that was a hopeless joke. Ferget it. The name's Tom and if you tell me what you need or what to do, I can help you.'

She points to the ice cream tracks on her arm. 'Drippin...see?' Shane laughs and points to the lines of chocolate dripping from her elbow onto the pavement. Then she buries her face in her coat.

'Kerry!' a rat-faced kid – looks about 14 – busts in. 'Kerry! Whut are ya doin!'

'You know her?'

'It's me fucken sister mate.'

'Shane,' I reassure her, 'Your brother's here.'

'Bruvvah!' she looks up.

'You're not Kerry!' says rat-face. And vanishes.

'Shane, ker-ryst! I KNOW what's happening but we can't stay here because the cops'll nab you. Walk or something'. Some old drunk asks me for two bob, I give it. 'Just try standing up and walkin a bit.'

She does like I asked and says, 'Thirteen pigs now.'

'What do you mean?'

'Thirteen pigs on foot patrol.'

'Please Shane, you look like shit. You're gonna get run over, arrested or somethin. Chuck the fucken ice cream and get some coffee'. I snatch the cone ('Hey, that's mine!') and chuck it in the gutter. 'Lemme wipe your arm.' I wash her in the Fountain and get chocolate stains on my Modshirt, damn.

'His name is Owen,' she says, deep in thought. Then she wants her Thing back. 'Where's my thing?'

'In the gutter, I threw it away. I'll buy you a coffee instead.'

Please jesus god krishna shiva buddha ac bhaktivedanta swami prabhupada get me out of this – save this dirty ugly blonde from being run over or locked up. Salli, if you could goddamn see me now. Mum, Janet, teachers and everyone else who says I don't care nothin about nuthink – I care!

'Here, have a smoke.'

'I need one darlin. Can I take one?'

'Here,' I open the pack. We take about 20 steps and she flops down in the first doorway. I sit too. She hands me her remainin flowers. The cig drops from her fingers.

'Owen,' she says. I hand back the flowers and put my arm around her shoulders.

'I'm not Owen.'

'Owen…uh…this ole guy gave me these flairs an said I was so pretty an there's nuthin prettier than a bunch of daff-dills…'

I correct her, 'Carnations'.

'An he give em to me ole George did.'

'Who's George? I thought he was Owen.'

'Naa, Owen's someone else. Who are YOU?'

‘I’m Tom.’

‘I’m Shane.’ We shake. ‘Uh where d’you say we were goin? Gimme a cig…where did you say we were goin darlin? How bout… she points a little way down the road, a place called Sweethearts. ‘Jess there…’.

It’s a tricky 50-yard journey. The same kinda uh-talk that doan make no sense, but when we get inside Sweethearts Shane spots someone she knows. She yanks my arm yells out, ‘Di!’ and says to me, ‘here’.

We slide into a semi-circular booth. Di comes straight over, so I’m trapped in a booth with Shane on one side and Di on the other. They lean across me and talk in a half-whisper which I don’t take notice of, cos it’s not for me. All I’m trying to figure out is, *are they pros?*

Di looks me over when she’s ready and doesn’t do any of this ‘is he suss?’ stuff. It’s like, ‘he must be okay cos you brung him Shane’ - so I must be okay. Then it’s what’s yer name stuff between me an Di while Shane whacks her head on the table and shuts her eyes.

‘You live around here?’ asks Di.

‘I live with my parents but a friend has a flat in Farrell Street.’

‘Hmm. Who’s your friend?’

‘A guy called Stu.’

‘How come you still livin at home?’

‘I’m finishin high skool. But ah gotta band.’

‘Well,’ says Di, indicating to a waitress, ‘Make the most of home an skool. The Cross can be bloody tough.’

‘I thought everybody’d understand in this place…’.

‘Nobody understands a thing, cept money.’ Abruptly, Di turns her attention back to Shane. Squeezes her hand. ‘You’re buggered mate,’ she says. A waitress with a Hungarian accent takes our order.

‘Di…?’ I ask, ‘Can I ask you something?’

‘What about?’

‘Well…what do I do about Shane?’

She leans back, crosses her arms, flicks me up-and-down, sez, ‘What have you got in mind?’

‘No, no…’ I begin awkwardly, ‘…I’m not actually sure what’s goin on. I just wanna help.’

‘Well kid,’ she replies, ‘Just keep doin what yer doin. You can’t help Shane. And you can’t help me on a bad night. I’m not actually sure *why* you want to get involved but that’s okay’.

I start saying something about the value of every human being when Di suddenly punches Shane on the arm and blurts, ‘Shake!’

Two guys who look like boxers walk in, givin everyone in the place the once-over. Tall guys, short-cut leather jackets, short hair, they check every booth and go: *yeah, you pass.* Then they spot us.

They flash a *'we've spotted em'* look and saunter over, thumbs in their belt buckles, wawkin slow like *Ear we cum.*

'Ready for this?' Di shakes a startled Shane, who raises her head from the table and does her physical best to straighten up. *Ker-yst!*

Allo allo. One two. One sits beside Di, the other next to Shane - blocking both exits. And I'm fair in the middle.

'Allo girls. H'war you Shane?'

'Uh?'

'Missed ya Wednesday…?'

'Yeah, uh sorry…that's because I ah…'.

'Come again?'

'Cos I've got this ah kidney infection, which was why…' plonk. Down she goes, her head hits the table.

Inside I'm going *hell, god, aaagh, sweetjesus!* But Shane crashing out face first and bleedin from the nose isn't registering with the others in the same big deal way as to me. When she gets her head back up it's all a bit - what else would you expect on a Saturday night at the Cross?

'Get up,' says the cop next to her, making way for Shane to stand in the aisle. The other coffee drinkers barely look up. He frisks her, asks for somethin to be outed from her boob pocket. It's a key. He asks for something else from another pocket. Nothing of interest either. Says she can sit now.

There's a long silence then the other one says, 'Stand up Di,' and he frisks her.

Then it's me.

'We haven't seen your long-haired friend before?' says Mr Crewcut, tipping my cigs all over the table. Some of them get wet of course, so he does the same with my matches.

'He's just some guy…', says Di.

'Some guy eh? Well I figured that out all by my fucken self! What's yer name?'

'Me?'

'Yeah dickhead – you.'

'Why?' I reply a bit smartarsed, like talking to a teacher, only this isn't a teacher, it's someone who grabs my wrist, squeezes it, stares into my eyes like *fuckyoukid when I ask you something don't hesitate*.

'Ow!'

In his own time, he releases the grip.

'I'm Tom.'

'Tom fucking *whut* stupid?'

'Truscott.'

'He lives with his parents,' says Di.

'Where?'

'Turramurra.'

The cop leans back in his seat, repeats 'Turramurra' and chuckles. And then to cap it Di adds, 'He's still at skool'. Why'd she say that? I wanna stand with Di and Shane.

'Have you ever been in trouble with the police before tonight?' he leers.

'No.'

'Then why are you looking fer it tonight? You don't look like a junkie to me.' Long pause.

Satisfied, he stands to leave and so does the other one. Saving the best cut til last. The cop that was beside Di rests both hands on the table, greases Shane out and says, 'We picked Owen up tonight.'

'Noooo!' Shane shrieks.

'Thought you'd enjoy that…' and they swagger out, the second cop flicking me a warning nod on his way out.

Di puts her head in her hands and says, 'That's my second time tonight'.

'You mean anywhere, any time, you can be searched?'

'Yep – strip-searched if they're in the mood.'

'Is that legal?'

'Maybe/maybe not. Wanna argue with em?'

Di calls for more coffee and we discuss streetlife.

I can't ask 'are you pros?' Neither can I ask, 'What's smack like? How do you buy it? What do you do with it when you've got it? Don't you care someday it'll kill you? Can I see a needle? What's the spoon for?' I can't ask those questions. I just can't.

After another cig Di says, 'If you still feel like helping, see Shane makes it home. I give you the cab fare.'

'Where does she live?'

'Forbes Street.'

'Just take it,' says Di, when I decline the note. 'And buy some cigs too.'

'Is she gonna be all right?'

'Give it an hour or so and she will. Don't worry, she's not gonna die on ya.' She gives Shane a bit of a shake, 'Shane…Shane…wakey wakey.'

'Uh…? Are they uh gone?'

'Yeah, and Tom's gonna see you home. Do like he sez and get off the streets, okay?'

'Yeah…uh.'

i saw the best minds of my generation vanishcompared to the value of the ugly frisked blonde who is so beautiful to me with dead carnations muttering owen owenwhereareyou tonight owen. who saidshe had a lesbian lady in pentridge and sucked her thumb like ababysaying I told mymothercheck-out-chick not this. who said she loved di like a sister both having fucked so many men that they can't remember numbers faces or names and all the sex they know is drysex or small pleasure inbetween a fix having a humanbodylike mineputtingarms about her shouldersor like old george saying you're pretty. christ! can'tsomeone see that love and respect is enough to get you off any jabbed needle but when i say it it'slike some suburban answer, when in truth there might be noanswer at all, just smack. me alone with her in a cab thinking shane i love you, you belongtome i believe. witnesses witness this, my heart going out like i've never seen it in a hard year. why do i want to eat her like poison. nothing's a joke anymore. faggot ballet dancer can bloody-up his wrists so i can tell my friends on monday, not you please shane. mother. mother in bed asleep wondering where your son is.
mother, i won't never ever take smack.

'I got some uh stuff sent from uh Newcastle. Hope you doan mind,' says Shane as she lets me into her flat, holding hands.

'I don't mind anything Shane that you do.'

Thinks: fucken smack.

Glad that bloody bastard Owen got nailed. I've damn well figured out who he is. He's the dirty pusher isn't he? Dragged you down you damn ugly princess dragged you down.

'What do you know about drugs, Tom?' She sits me down among the sacks. Stolen stuff.

'Dammit, I know *nuthin*. I doan know nuthin about LSD, nuthin about grass, nuthin about smack. Nuthin about nothing. And because everything here is so bloody *real,* don't know if I need to find out more'.

She ain't listenin. She's rummagin through those sacks, pullin out stuff, sayin she'll make coffee, callin me darlin, sayin look at this it's a statue of the buddha, or look at this dress – cept there's six of them, identical.

Sacks is all she's thinkin about and what's in them. I can't regain her attention but I want something more than what I want from Salli, Janet or Irene.

This moment is Art.

To me.

'Where did you live before comin here?' I ask.

Rummage, rummage, rummage. Then, 'Bulladelah – heard of it?'

'No.'

'Well,' she says, 'that's where I lived'. She pulls out silks, cups, trinkets, wraparounds, bracelets, plastic things, Indian beads, Asian things, new all new. Looks like the contents of a hippie shop.

Can I get your attention please?

I cain't believe what I'm seein. Shane's eyes are back in their sockets. Her skin is losing that sick shine. She's wiped the vomit from her bottom lip. And now that she's taking her clothes off and trying on dresses, I can see she's got a terrific chape.

'Doan go yet darlin. Tell me what you think about THIS!' She turns her back, strips to black panties, slips into a short red satin dressing-type gown with dragon patterns and turns around. 'Like ut?'

'Lovely,' I reply, trying not to sound like suddenly she is to me the most beautiful woman I've ever met.

'You look great, but I really should head back Shane. I doan know where all that stuff came from but I've got to get back to Stu's because someone got hurt there before I met you'.

'Just sit still for a minute darlin. Ten more minutes and I'll be through.'

I do like she says and doze off. Doan know what time it is any more. Feels like the longest day.

'Look at this card darlin!' I wake with a jolt. 'I got ut for my bruvver who's in Long Bay...'

'I gotta go…'.

'Hey,' she says, comin close. And I can't remember the old dribbly Shane any more. 'You were real nice to me Tom. Saw me safe. Why did you bother with me?'

'Because you were in trouble. Am I a real person to you, at last?' I reply.

She leads me to her bed, lies me down and strokes my tired brain. In her arms, I feel strangely free, as if this is the Moment.

This is when I'm not 6th Form, not Turramurra, not a Blitz, not a longhair, not a poet, not a I-just-met-Dobell kinda guy. I'm actually just as I am and there's almost no turning back.

Love is not a poem or a dream or a lie or a myth or a promise. It's a small breast peeking out from a red satin dragon dressing gown and a wet tongue-kiss. I'm so happy.

Shane undoes the buttons of my shirt, removes it. Undoes my belt buckle, unzips my fly and holds my frightened cock in her right hand.

This is the only woman in my life who might say it's all right if I do it all the time, a little bit or never. I love this woman. I squeak the words: *I've never done this before*.

I know my responsibilities. This is the Great Moment when I change into Roger Ramjet. I've got to know where to put it. Make her cum four times.

Be a man. Do position 62, 69, 137 plus the missionary position like a fucken superstud. I've seen James Bond films.

I know the score. I'm expected to leave her gasping. It's a Real Man's job in a Hero's world.

'I don't know if I can do this Shane,' I tell her, looking into her eyes.

'It's okay darlin,' she says. 'I'll help you.'

13
I'm A Man

After
Shane
skool
seems
ridiculous.

WE'D LOVE TO
TURN
YOU

14

Sgt Peppers Lonely Hearts Club Band

The Blitz have got a party gig. And we're hot to trot. Pity we're not gettin paid.

We play *Glad All Over*-type stuff in the first set.

In our second set Jay lashes out a few lead breaks in our 12-bar Blues in E. I make up on-the-spot lyrics, like:

Mark is playing bass guitar
Bob he's playing drums
Jay is playing lead guitar
And me – (something something) - strums
I got them blues boy, I got them blues in E
This is 1967, we can be anything we want to be
Let me hear that bluesboy moan…!

Third set we get vicious. Veeeecious. We slam into *My Generation,* which – apart for those tricky bass lines – goes perfect. I play solo *Satisfaction,* just me on flatstick thrash guitar and Mark singin. Next *Communist Girls,* followed by *The Loved One* and two Easybeat songs. They all go crazy wantin an encore, so we do another 12-bar blues song, not entirely dissimilar to the previous one:

Salli she's my friend
Pity she ain't here
Something something something
Something something beer
I got them blues boy, I got them blues in A
Do yourself a favour
Everyone get out my way
Play that lead, bluesboy, yeah…!

After that we invite anyone who can play an instrument (or hit a can) to get up and jam. So it's *Blues in A Jam* followed by *Blues Jam in E.* Then *Extended Superjam in A.* Also, *Blues Jam in E with capo on the 1st fret.* I get sick of the same old 12-bars and launch into a made-up version of *Gloria:*

I drive around here
Just abaaaart midnight
Makes you feel so cool man
Makes you feel all right
And you spell it H-O-L-D-E-N
H-O-L-D-E-N (Holden)
White Holden panel van.

Then some skinny little drunk wants to get up and sing Presley numbers.

'Of course ya mean Reg Presley of the Troggs?'

'Naah, Elvis the King.'

'Never rerd of im!'

I glance at Bob who gives me the nod. We slip offstage leaving Mark and Jay to sort out the Presley caper.

The drunk guy grabs the mike and goes, *Warn fer da murney.* No back-up. Nuthin. (I feel like grabbin the mike and doing the Pope joke.) He goes, *Two fur da show!* Mark and Jay still do nothing. *Three to git ready…*Mark and Jay put their instruments down and walk off. Some oldie in a Hawaiian shirt takes the mike from the Presley-guy and says, *How bout a few party jokes! Today's teenagers are alike in many disrespects…!* Ha ha ha. *Behind every successful man there stands a surprised mother-in-law…!* Ha ha har.

He doesn't get much further when another oldie, this one in a safari suit, takes over the mike and announces the reason we've all 'gathered here' is because his daughter (the one with the flickups sitting in the Morticia Addams chair) has turned 21 today. Yay! He says something about giving her the 'key to the door' and that *she has stopped asking where she came from and refuses to say where she is going!* Boom boom. The Presley guy yells something out that I don't get. Possibly obscene, cos no one laughs. Then comes all sorts of catcalls and boring anecdotes about her first boyfriend, the time she did something embarrassing on a bus when she was six and how cute she was in nappies. The Morticia girl looks like she doesn't know where to hide.

She should try under here with me and Cherie. Me and Bob have found two blankets and two girls who reckon the Blitz wuz *Grrreat.* Mine sez her ole man is a cop and her favourite band is a Melbourne group called the Kinetics. She's kissed the lead singer which makes me & him equal.

'Hey! You sly dog!' The blanket gets ripped off us. It's Stu! Stu arrives with a dozen tinnies and a girl in tow. I peer into the dark and…cripes – it's Shane. How did Stu get to meet her? (Both live around the Cross, I guess.)

'Shane!'

'Hey Tom, H'war ya darlin?' We kiss each other hello, me wishing she was with anyone else but Stu. (She's in enough trouble.) But you can't babysit anyone for more than a couple of hours and they can't babysit you either - I think – taking a glance at Cherie.

'Shane, remember that night when…?' Ah, never mind. She kisses me once more, calls me darlin and that's it.

Stu takes over, 'I'm a mess. Got totally destroyed last night'.

'Where'd you go?'

'Dunno – where'd we go Shane?'

Shane says they went to Les Girls where they don't have to pay cos she knows the doorman.

'How come you go to joints like that instead of seeing bands?' I can't understand anyone going anywhere cept music venues.

'Fuck off', says Stu. 'You're always on about bands'. Then to Shane, 'Where'd we go after Les Girls? I forget. *Really…!*'

'Saw a band,' she laughs at him. She's looking fine tonight.

'Which band?' I ask Stu.

'Christ I dunno! Who gives a fuck! I'm trying to fucken talk.' He greases me right out, then back to his story. 'No...we went somewhere where I had three drinks.'

'How'd Quince pan out?'

'Why d'you keep int'ruptin. Quince happened ages ago. He moved out. But last night we went somewhere...?'

'...had 13 drinks,' Shane grins.

'Yeah.'

'Then,' says Shane, 'I asked this guy if he had any grass and he said yes. So we went out the back and he told me it was good grass. I said how much? And he sold me. I had *one* joint. Only one. Picked up my shoes, walked out and went to sleep in the car'.

'I sat on her,' says Stu. 'I got viciously pissed and when ah got in the car I forgot she wuz there.'

'And he sat on me!'

'Well, what are women for...ha, har!' Stu laughs.

Cherie is going, *who is this creep?* She's moving away with that are-these-really-your-friends expression on her dial.

'I wasn't half as pissed as I was stoned though,' Stu ha-ha-hars. 'I sat on her head!'

'What is it like...?' I ask, '...being stoned?'

'What sort of a fucken question's that?' Stu snaps.

Shane says, 'Like everything, it has to be experienced'.

'You're a fucken jerk!' Stu explodes in my face, 'Where's Jay? I came over to get Jay, where is he?'

'Over there with Mark and a couple of girls pro'bly.'

'Farken farken,' says Stu, to the disapproval of a few older guests. Then he spots Bob. 'Hey you! Blackfella...!' Stu hands him a beer but Bob backs off.

'What's with you prick?'

I stick my hand out, 'It's okay, I'll have it...' and Stu hands me the beer without lifting his eyes off Bob. Farken farken.

'Doan talk to me like that,' says Bob.

Stu doesn't care that he's attracted the attention of the party bouncer Mash Mularz, cousin to the Morticia Addams party girl. Mash puts his arm on Stu, friendly-like but firm and says, 'Cool it a bit'. Walks away. Doesn't hear Stu mutter, *Fucken Polack*.

Time for me to put in the good word for Bob, 'No one likes being put down Stu'.

'I didn't put him down, I just called him a *Fucken Abo* which he is.'

Oh god, Bob's still in earshot.

'Ferget Bob!' Shane cries out.

'She's right Stu,' I tell him, 'Leave Bob alone'. *Pick on us instead,*' But his focus has narrowed. Whatever is put before him is what Stu responds to now.

'Tom, you're not even worth picking on. Ker-ryst – *what's a joint like?* What are ya!'

Shane gets that I've-heard-it-all-before look and switches off. Somehow Cherie has wandered back into our circle. Stu claps his eyes on her and says, 'And what's YOUR name?'

'Cherie.'

'Cheryl. That's a bloody awful name. Another schoolkid – like im', he sticks his thumb at me.

'The name's Cherie not Cheryl and I work at the NRMA office in town.'

I take Cherie's hand, 'Let's go…'. Stu grabs my wrist, forces me back down and says, 'That's the fucken problem with you lot. One drink and you reckon you're pissed. Sit down and tawk.'

'What do you want to talk about Stu?'

'Well I can't talk to *you* about much. If you didn't have clothes, girls and music you wouldn't have anything to say. They ought to try teaching you something useful at school.'

'Like what?'

'Like how to place a fucken bet! I bet you haven't learned anything in 12 months. Go on – hit me?'

'Who wrote *Wuthering Heights?'*

'Who wrote fucken Wuthering Heights! Who fucken cares?' I think we've got Mash's attention again. ('Cut the language!')

The party is running down. Mark is trying to stop some drunk from using our gear. The birthday girl is being passed around and kissed happy birthday by all the ole guys and uncles who are going 'haw haw haw' and getting as much of a squeeze-up as they can jokingly manage. *Haw haw haw, c'm ear darlin and press against your Uncle Jerry who used to change your nappies when you were knee-high to a grasshopper.* 'Happy 21st!' goes some smelly drunk uncle or neighbour, passin the girl around like a bottle while their wives sip pink champagne and ignore the men cos that's what men are supposed to do to girls when they turn 21. It's a good ole boys custom. Can't mess with that.

Uncle Jerry is now having a spew. Mr Potter and his son are trying to dak him. They're grabbing his pants while he's bending over. Down go the pants. Har har. All the ole guys grab him then throw im in the swimming pool. Peels of laughter from the blokes, while the women sip and boast about their men's business successes.

'*Wuthering Heights…'* mocks Stu. 'Ask me something real. How you find a flat? How you get a job? Just fucken ask me useful you fucken skoolkid…?'

'Have you ever heard of Woody Guthrie?'

'See, I bloody told ya it's all music an skool. I know who Woody Guthrie is, he's a fucken Blues singer.'

'A Folk singer.'

'Folk singer, blues singer, pop singer…who cares?' he calls for more liquor. 'You couldn't survive if you left home. But you're *always* going on about peace & luv. I don't *think* about Vietnam, ever. And poetry. Who gives a shit about poetry? Vincent van Goff! Eric Clapton…' but when he gets to Jimi Hendrix he turns his gaze back on Bob.

'…Hendrix is just some nig that's cashing in!'

Oh no Stu, don't nigger him man.

'This one's no nigger,' he spits out the words in Bob's direction, not caring he's upsetting party people. Stu says, 'Niggers are American. This one's a *coon!'*

Snap.

Bob rushes in, fists up, but Stu's half-ready. He clips Bob on the chin. At first, Bob stands like a boxer, then he suddenly goes berserk – punching air, punching Stu's neck, now face and stomach again and again. Stu occasionally lands one, but Bob keeps coming until Stu starts defending himself. It's all he can do. The oldies spot the dust-up. Mash and some other guy race over and pull them apart. It takes two to pin Bob down, but not a lot for Stu to stop. 'You were fucken lucky…!' Stu growls. The bouncers take over and Shane is managing Stu – offering another beer of course. Then the birthday girl starts screaming, 'You're ruining my party!'

'It's your lucky night mate',' Stu shakes his fist. But he doesn't say 'Abo' and he doesn't say coon. Not this time.

Bob gives him the finger and turns away with contempt.

Just then Clayton comes whistling down the drive. Clayton, wearing a kaftan and looking like Jesus. He's got something under his arm. Not *Ulysses.* Not Kahlil Gibran's *The Prophet.* It's a record not a book.

He exclaims, 'Wait til you hear this!'

'What is it?' Cherie asks.

'The Beatles new album, *Sgt Peppers Lonely Hearts Club Band.'* Then he realises no one is smiling and says, 'What's going on?'

'Nuthen - Stu and Bob had a bit of a go.'

'I'll fucken kill im!' continues Stu, as Shane drags him into a cab. No one's interested. Not now that *Sgt Peppers* has arrived.

'Gis a look at the cover man…' Clayton hands me the album.

'Check it out!'

'Where'd you git it?'

'Play it!'

'Why's it called *Sgt Peppers?'*

'I get it,' says Cherie, reading the back cover lyrics and getting clever. '*Lucy in the Sky with Diamonds* is LSD. And this bit, *I'd love to turn you on*…it's about drugs! Wow! Isn't that trendy!'

'This album IS drugs,' announces Clayton. 'You don't need drugs when you've got *Sgt Pepper.'*

We all go inside, doing the midnight shift around the stereo, listening to *Sgt Pepper.* The girl with sun in her eyes. Cellophane flowers. Hogshead of real fire. Drank a cup. The wall of illusion. You're only very small. Love at first sight. Lots about love.

'What do you think true love is?' Cherie asks of me.

'I think true love is finding someone who never says NO to me and who I never say NO to. Say no just once and it's over.'

'Wow,' she says. 'Hand me the record?'

'No.'

Marmalade skies. Rocking horse people. Save the world. Stops my mind. Peace of mind. We're all One. Pray for me Rita Meter Maid, pray for me Lucy. Pray for me girl with kaleidoscope eyes. We're all in the Sgt Peppers Church of the Holy Duel of Song. Music is born again. Born into the best of times. Born into an age of reason. Born into the season of the witch. Born into the Season of Light.

If love is the answer, what's the question? I used to luv Shane but now I love Lucy. I love the Meter Maid. Maybe I even love my olds. In *She's Leaving Home* I imagine my parents sad-faced. And matriculated me packing my bags for Melbourne. Could even be Vietnam if the ballot gets me.

Hope I die before I get old is the opposite of *When I'm 64.* Imagine a 64-year old Beatle mending a fuse? I'm 64 in year 2013. Impossible!

'I'm not too sure about this record,' I confess to Bob.

'You don't like it?'

'I like it too much.'

'Whaddya mean?'

'I mean – whatever's going to happen to the songs *we* write now?'

'Yeah,' he replies thoughtfully. 'After *Sgt Peppers* there's nowhere for music to go. It's all over.'

15

You're Driving Me Insane

'Why do you wear your hair so long?' asks Dad.

'Why'd you wear that James Bond stuff?'

'Because that's how businessmen dress.'

'They're cocks.'

'Don't you swear at me young man!'

'Your friends swear.'

'That's different,' says Dad.

It always is.

Mum changes the subject. 'I've got another letter from Ken…'.

'I doan wanna hear anything about Vietnam,' I reply. I believe in Love cos of Clayton who lent me Gibran's *The Prophet* and I'm about to turn vegetarian. Maybe.

'He's coming home.'

'He should never have gone. I bet he's killed people.'

'Simply doing his duty.'

'Sucked in by the System. I'd rather shoot my toe off than go to war. If there was a war, I'd be sure to die Mum. People like me, who doan have the stomach for killing – they're first to die!'

'So you and your crowd would just allow the Communists overrun this country that we fought to defend.'

'*Thou shalt not kill* – that's from your Book!'

'Pity you didn't notice the other Nine Commandments!'

'Good thing too pro'bly that you and your friends *aren't* in the Army!' Dad contributes. 'I can't imagine anything more ridiculous than you, Clayton, Bob and Mark in jungle greens!'

'Anyway…' says Mum, '(I'm not being racist but) I can't see why you hang around with that Bob – he's a half-Aboriginal!'

'Yeah, a real Australian!'

'An Australian?' says Dad, pulling off his after-work tie, 'You can't seriously call a Blackman an Australian! They don't even vote!'

'And that's unfair. We're not racially prejudiced like your generation!'

'Hang about - I heard your friend joking about Spags. And we all hate the Ruskies, c'mon – you can only trust yer own.'

No, I can't trust anybody! 'Our generation is different,' I tell him, 'we think the Abos are okay'.

'So do we,' he replies confidently. 'Your grandfather was a woodcutter in the Hunter Valley. And he never *ever* mistreated them. He worked alongside em and even drove em to church. So what's the prob?'

The phone rings.

Dad picks up the phone and pulls a face, 'It's the Police'.

Mum flashes a terrified look at me. Like, *what can I have done? It must be drugs!* That panic moment. I can read all over her face.

I'd love to turn you off.

I hand Mum the Kahlil Gibran book. 'I believe in that Mum. Our generation believes in love not war. And once yer dead, yer gone - that's how it'll be Jesus-wise. Money doesn't matter. Put the word FREE in front of everything. Free love. Free land. Free food. Free university. Free…dom!

'Shuddup!' says Dad urgently. Then he says YES five times down the line, clicks down the receiver and glares at me.

I doan know why he's looking at me that way. I haven't done anything. But Dad still looks me over as if there's something terribly wrong with me as a person. 'Your mate Stu and his accomplice have been arrested for breaking and entry,' he announces.

'Whaaat?'

'He's down at the Hornsby Police Station. They want bail. That's why he phoned.'

'When did this happen?' I stammer. 'Who's his *accomplice* – not Jay!'

'Someone called Shane. They took her straight to hospital. Who do you know called Shane?'

'His girlfriend or something...'

'To think that boy has the gall to ask you to put up the bail money!' blurts Mum. 'Did you tell him he's dreamin!'

'Actually no,' says Dad, clearing his throat. 'I said I'd be there in 15 minutes'.

'What on earth promoted you to say yes?' she asks.

'I like Stu,' Dad replies. 'And I like Tom's fiends, if only they'd cut their hair and stop playing those bloody awful records!'

16

Tales of Brave Ulysses

Teachers tell me I will amount to nuthin even though I'm the smartest kid in Ancient History class. I can also paint, play guitar and write poems. From Mr Kennedy, I've borrowed the *Letters of Vincent van Gogh* written mostly to his brother Theo. Ker-ryst! I'm the only one in my class who seems to know about that stuff. Oh, they all know Vincent's an artist, but not much else. Yet I'm the nobody and the nuthin. The same applies to Mark, same for Bob.

Mark looks a bit like a fashionplate. He's fine at Maths and Science and could probably do okay at anything that doesn't bore him. Another loser, according to the teachers. Bob can play tuba, bass, 6-string guitar, drums and a bit of harmonica. He wrote a pretty good tune to *Communist Girls,* which again counts for nuthin. And he's got no real probs with his schoolwork. Another shithead. The three of us have been told we'll never get proper jobs because of our lousy goddamn attitudes.

MEANWHILE. (And I'm not making this up...) This is dead true. A guy in the class below us actually screwed an Alsatian. The boss tells me that the dog-screwer is the kind of guy the staff really respects, which figures.

Two 4th Formers dropped acid last weekend in a park in Eastwood. Not that these guys are exactly popular with the teachers, but it wasn't *them* who copped a big lecture on drugs. That was me.

All these kids get fair-to-good report cards. Their parents never get phoned up and told that their kids are bent – which I supposedly am. Plus I've never seen any of these guys standing outside the Boss's office for an hour at a stretch, and I've never heard the Boss call them good-for-nothing juvenile delinquent types. Just us. I'm walkin along the school verandah, pretty pleased with my Ancient History grade and thinking of a new girl called Debbie when John invites me to a game of chess. So we do that while eating sandwiches. I win, as usual, and then we talk about all sorts of stuff that is pretty obscene coming from a prefect like him. But it's okay coming from me, because I am a good-for-nothing juvenile delinquent type.

Some form-oners are scrapping not far from where we're sitting, and John – being a prefect – leaves the chessboard and approaches them. Seeing him, they squeak and run into the locker room. John follows, but I can't be bothered, sitting here quietly thinking about Vietnam, Vincent, Mr Kennedy and probably Ulysses.

Then a fifth former runs past, looking a bit excited, as if he's been given the word. And another guy runs to the locker room as well. I guess if there's something happenin in the boy's locker room, I wouldn't want to miss out. So I stand up, make a big thing about yawning and amble along the verandah, careful to avoid Mr Devlin who is sure to check the colour of my socks. There's a crowd of kids cheering and - being senior - I push them out of my way so I can see what's going on. I can't figure it out. All I see is a 4th former called Louie, drinking something.

'Hey Pye, what's happenin?'

'Louie is drinking something.'

I can see that.

'It's 76% proof alcohol,' says a 4th former called Bryson, watching Louie take another swig from something I've never seen in a bottle shop. More! More!

'Any takers?' says Louie, gasping for breath and swinging the bottle.

Well, Mark can't be here, otherwise he'd hook in.

'I'll have a go!' I shout out and am instantly promoted to the front row. Louie passes me the bottle. Is this a challenge?

Louie's got a band and his two band mates are standing either side of him, like bodyguards or something. Anyway, I've got the bottle, take a deep breath and gulp. *Eeech!*

Cheers and laughter. Someone yells, 'Go!' So it's back to Louie. He stands, legs apart, raises his left hand and brings the bottle to his lips with the right. Slurp! Cheers! 76% alcohol-proof! Yay!

My turn.

These schoolkids must be pretty bored to be watching this like a chicken fight. They're just thrilled by the word 'alcohol'. There's really nothing to it. So - just to show off - I pick out a little 1st former and tell him to take a pull. Not wanting to disobey a 6th former, he brings it to his lips and is so shocked that he almost drops the bottle. Back to me V Louie. My turn. His turn. My turn. His. Cheers, yowls, hoots, then the bell goes and everyone skuttles off to class and I forget the whole incident. I'm in Modern History class when some kid called Charlene interrupts the class and says I've got to go to the Deputy Headmaster's office – my Ancient History teacher, Mr Calder.

What can this be about? I borrow Mark's comb to make my hair look shorter and head for the office. Calder likes me. I am his only Level One student (everyone else in the class is doing Level Two Ancient History) and because I am so disruptive in other classes, that Calder has tamed me makes him look good. So I walk along the verandah, past the Alsatian guy and up to the school secretary and ask, 'What's this all about?' She ignores me, of course.

Here we go again…standing outside an office, which is how I spend hours and hours (my father pays private school fees for this). But after only about three minutes, Calder opens his office door and says 'enter'. For him, I stand more casually than I do for the Boss, because I'm his Level One student, etc…

'You've been reported for drinking alcohol in the locker room,' he announces.

'Oh?' (Just me of course, not Louie. Not that I want Louie to get done, in fact I'll cover for him. It's just weird the whole alcohol incident is all about me.)

'True?'

I think through the faces in the locker room crowd. Who could have put me in? John was the only prefect there, but he'd never have dobbed. Who else? Louie's 4th form crowd – nope - cos they'd risk Louie getting in trouble. Not the juniors either. And then I remember that fucken Carter guy – a wannabe prefect still in 5th form. It's gotta be him.

'Yes sir, it's true.'

I can see from the way Calder lowers his eyes that he was hoping for, 'Nope, it's a heap of crap. (You're thinking of someone who isn't coming 1st in your Ancient History class)'. But I tell im yes. Disappointed, nevertheless doing his job, Calder draws himself to his full height and pronounces sentence. 'Tom, drinking on school grounds is an expellable offence. I will be referring this to the headmaster. I have no choice.' I can hear the Boss screaming at some kid in the next room. Then *Twack.* And *twack* again, followed by more abuse. 'You disreputable…' etc.

Expulsions aren't like that, not noisy. Yelling is reassuring actually. It means that kid is still part of the group and about to return to class. Jimmy Fingers got expelled last year, cos stealing was his thing. Jimmy said when you get expelled the Boss phones your parents first. They know before you do. Then you get called up, called in and told. That's all that happens. That's everything. They don't check your hair, your uniform, you don't get called a *hopeless degenerate.* None of that.

Calder and I contemplate what might have been. There goes his Level One glory. It's okay, I understand. He's GOT to tell the Boss.

'That's it then,' he shrugs. 'Get the bottle.'

So I walk out the office, get snarled at by the school secretary, walk down the stairs, along the verandah, into the Boy's Locker Room, reach into the bin and it's still there. The empty 76% proof bottle. Back to Calder's office and I don't have to wait. Straight in. 'Here it is,' I hand him the bottle.

He reads the label, looks up and says, 'It's *medicine!',* pauses in thought, looks back at me and says. 'Get out of here. Go back to class.'

I LOVE P.J. PROBY BECAUSE
HE IS BETTER than all the DULL Boys
I KNOW, All the DISC JOCKEYS SAY he is GAS
and FAB and WILD and TOO MUCH for the
HUMAN MIND! and He must BE IMPORTANT and he
WEARS this FAB GEAR. none of the Boys I know dress
like THAT and I threw a STREAMER at HIM and it
TOUCHED HIM and I'm SURE HE wiggled
at ME
AND
as soon as
I got home
I wrote him
a letter
saying HOW
I loved Him
AND WOULD DO
ANYTHINK FOR
HIM and HOW
I DREAM of making
LOVE To HIM...
Oh I'm being
AWFUL going on
like this... WOT
would RINGO SAY!
I LOVE YOU P.J.P.
PJ
PROBY
PROBE
PROBE
PROBY
P.J.
P.J.
PJ
PRO
P.J.

17

I Dig Rock N Roll Music

Never never NEVER respect the system no matter what it says or does, never never never respect.

Love. You can luv.

Learn. You can lurn.

But never never NEVER respect its stupid principles and ideas. Why should you? The system doesn't respect you & me.

I think about these aspects of life a lot. More than the oldies credit me for.

I think about leadership. Prime ministership. Pop starship. I think about fame. I think about teachership. Prefectship. Parenthood. Bossism. Systemites. I think about having a say. And I'm not so stupid.

Why do the oldies think we're shitheads when the juniors think we're hip? They copy the way me and Mark bend our uniform and they copy our hair. They walk and talk like mini-us and listen to music we've approved of. Therefore, why do the olds think we're such failures, when these kids all think we're terrific?

Teachers pull rank all the bloody time. They cane you – bend you over and slash the back of your legs until you cry especially if you're in junior school. And if you don't register pain they keep doing it until you bloody well show you're hurt. Only then are they happy.

They give you six – then a seventh – maybe an eighth for a separate reason. That's how they keep their numbers up (cos six is the legal limit): they cane you for separate offences. That whiplash sting across the back of your legs, across your fingers or across your arse, delivered with all that teacher's smiling might. The young male teacher, thumbs in his belt buckle, laughing at you, calling you a coward because it hurts so much you wish to god you could strangle him because he nightmared you in front of the whole class.

That shame.

That humbling.

That apology he wrings out of you because he's so tough while you're artistic and sensitive. Once he sees that in you he thinks ahhh I can do society a favour by breaking the spirit of this young Mod with strange hair and non-regulation socks.

My ole man didn't hit me at home but he sent me to a skool that built a religion out of it.

You guessed it, I got caned again yesterday.

They don't usually cane 6th formers but they caned me.

They caned me because I wouldn't march around the quadrangle when they had the 'marching' period. I wouldn't march because I hate the whole military thing. I hate going left-right left-right left-right. I hate taking orders from shitheads like Wilson and Devlin. Even before the seven cuts, the conformity of marching seemed so cruel to my spirit. When I march left-right left-right I feel they're breaking something inside me. Yet they reckon it's good for me. Whereas I feel that if I say YES to marching I'm saying yes to something much bigger.

I can't respect myself when I march. It's more important than it appears. It's as if – if I march around the quadrangle - I stop believing my beliefs. How can I sing in a band when someone in the audience might yell out, 'I saw yer march in sport uniform!' To be a person who I respect I mustn't march around the quadrangle in terrible shorts.

They thrashed me.

So I marched.

How can an unworthy like me put Howlin Wolf on the turntable? How can I play John Lee Hooker? How can I sensibly talk to Mr Kennedy about Vincent when I marched left/right.

Jay's a very good friend. I dig im as much as Mark and Bob and Clayton and Salli. I've got to stop saying that. Instead of saying 'I dig im' I've got to say 'I luv im'. I love Jay. Love is in.

Jay's straight with me. He knows I'm hopeless on guitar and that when I'm writing words and going 'let's all be creative man' that I'm diverting attention from not even being a half-decent guitarist.

Jay's square-on. I mean - he's no saint. He'd root a rat with a harelip but there's even something honest about the way he does that. There's something down-to-earth about Jay's drinking and wannafuck attitude that I respect. He's been a bit mixed-up since his father died. But he's a fair dinkum guy who I don't reckon would march around the quadrangle even if he were at skool, no matter how hard they caned him. (Or, maybe no one ever caned him hard enough. They did me.)

And now – if there is a god – I want every teacher who every laid an angry finger on me to burn in hell just like the Bible has promised. I want eternal fires to burn their skin right off. I want their pain to be endless. I want to hear them shriek for mercy that never comes because they *chose* to whip me and my friends across the back of the knees with a thin bamboo stick that broke those little veins that you can see here. But I can't tell my parents about all this caning because I've got long hair, play in a band and I'm on the wrong side of the Vietnam question.

Sometimes I don't like my life but I can't quite put the finger on what I doan like about it.

*

‘Hey Salli…!’ cos Salli’s waiting at the bus stop. ‘Do you wanna come with me to a band practice then to a gig?’

‘You’ve never had a decent gig before?’

‘A gig in Redfern. Fer reel. Stu got it for us before goin back to Melbourne.’

‘Turramurra can’t ever play Redfern,’ she mocks.

‘Maybe I’ll take Irene then…’

‘She thinks you’re a creep.’

‘Come on Salli, it’s our first proper gig and I’d like you there…’

She shrugs, so it must be a ‘date’.

‘You know what I’d like to do?’

‘What?’

‘A chant.’

‘Sounds good.’

‘I’d like us to put down all instruments, pick up percussion things like bin lids and beer cans and chant the words of the Buddha, whatever they are…’

‘Other than you not being Buddhist, it’s probably a great idea. I can’t see why you play all that Swin-Ger-pop.’

‘Because it gets em dancing. C’mon Salli, don’t bag me out – I wanna write songs with Bob. I wanna get a sax player in there…’

‘Who?’

‘Someone Bob knows.’

‘Okay Tom, I’ll keep you company.’

Suddenly I want to kiss her. More importantly I really want Salli to see this gig because it’s Redfern and anyone who pulls a Redfern gig has got to have some cred. I need her to help me stretch.

Please approve of me, goddamn.

Clayton pulls up in his FJ and Salli & I pile in. Clayton, with a mouth harp in his pocket and John Lennon’s new book on the dash. (*Treasure Ivan* and *Captain Smellit.)* He runs us to Jay’s place where we set up for rehearsal.

We give *Communist Girls* our best shot and it works. Then I get enthusiastic about freeform songs because Salli’s here for support. Jay tells us a hitchhiking yarn instead. We wrangle about Dave Clark Five songs, with me dead against them (with Salli in the room). Mark threatens to walk out cos he’s sick of being in a band that always argues. Jay, who’s attended the Mob’s rehearsals says, *what band doesn’t?* Then Samantha’s name comes up and Salli arks right up. *Bitch!* Mark again threatens to walk out if Salli doesn’t shut up. I take her side of course. He slags her out, unplugs his guitar and asks me to choose between him or her. But she's had enough and storms out reckoning that any band with Mark in it has just gotta suck.

I chase after her but the damage has bin done. I race back to the band room where everyone's drinking beer cept Bob, who's picked up a guitar.

He plays his own song called *Never Let the System Get To You.*

Never let the system get to you my friend
Never let the system show what it can do…

'What's that chord Bob?' asks Mark.

'An E7+1.'

'A whut?'

'An E7 with a G note in it.'

'Why don't you play guitar a bit more Bob?'

'I do. This is the only place I play drums.'

'Why doan we try a few more originals maybe…?' questions Mark, constantly glancing at me, guilty-like for pissing Salli off.

My opportunity! 'I've got some lyrics right here called *Suburban Women…!*'

'Shurrup,' says Jay, 'it's Bob's turn. What else has he got?'

'Ahh shit!' I exclaim, 'I can't find the lyrics…'

'Shut up Tom – go on Bob…?'

'Well…' Bob says kinda quietly, '…here's one I wrote called *This Is It.* Pick up on it if you can, it's got a G-A-E thing in there…'

Every President's a hero, every Red hates being free
And the Irish hate each other, they're no threat to you and me
While the gods of truth and justice keep the peace in Vietnam
Grab the diamonds for the greedy from a broken black blood hand
This is it. This is it. This is it.

Well I'm playing with a puzzle and I don't know how it fits
It's a game called World War 3 and I think that this is it

They've been fighting for the Holy Land forever and a day
Not a word from their Messiah, just a whispered CIA
We'll let cowboys run the planet and computers take our place
If our future is a jackboot stamping down on baby's face
This is it. This is it. This is it

Well I'm playing with a puzzle and I don't know how it fits
It's a game called World War 3 and I think that this is it

'Wow!' says Jay.

'That's a helluva song!' says Mark.

'Good news guys! I've found the lyrics to *Suburban Women!*'

But they're not in'trested.

*

We rush through our standards, pack the gear and head over the Bridge to Redfern. Me – wishing Salli was here. Mark – wishing Samantha was too. And Bob – staring out the window thinking about Louise.

Two cars – Clayton's FJ and Jay's Mum's Morris 1100. Redfern, here we come. Three amps, three guitars, one drumkit, two mikes, two mike stands, a song list and bloody gaffa tape.

*

We find the place and start unloading. 'Hey Neil!' yells Jay.

Neil is a Dutch blues harp player with an Aboriginal girlfriend. He saunters over and starts by testing Clayton's harmonicas. 'Good harp,' he says, 'Make sure you have a blow.' Clayton doesn't answer cos all he can play is *Man of Constant Sorrow.*

'Where do we set up?' I ask.

'Over here mate, follow me,' says Neil jostling people out of his way and pointing to the corner in the main bar. No stage. No lights. Just a corner like he said. We have to walk through – shove thru - the audience to get on and off stage.

I head back to the cars and exclaim, 'Hey guys, have you taken a look inside!'

'Not yet.'

'It's packed full of Abos. Only a coupla Whiteys!'

There's a moment of silence broken by Jay who says, 'That's all right, all they want's a good time. Anyway, we've got Bob!'

'Yeah but...we're the minority!'

'I know the feeling,' says Bob a tad harshly.

So we carry in the gear, pushing through the audience – s'cuse, s'cuse, s'cuse – and a short guy wearing a workshirt hits me with a big rave about Kempsey while I'm still holding an amp - otherwise his rave might have bin half-in'tresting. 'Sore right mate,' he suddenly realizes, 'I'll give you a hand'. He carries it for me then says, 'Wanna beer?'

We set up cept for Bob. He can't get away because people keep coming up to him and shaking his hand, asking him whether he's Garigal, which he reckons he isn't. Someone asks his mother's name. He replies, 'Barbara'.

One thing about these black guys is they all want to talk to you or help you. And it's always guys, even though there's heaps of women in the pub. Meanwhile Clayton's off in a corner asking all sorts of questions about the Dreamtime. At first, I don't think they know what he's on about, then one guy starts about the Rainbow Serpent which is exactly what Clayton wants to hear.

'There's Sacrid Sites in Sydney…' I overhear one say. (Well – I carn't help but think – Sydney? - that's damn near impossible! But what would I know?)

'They got a big mob out there…' I hear him continue.

'Yeah yeah,' Clayton replies, 'I dig'.

'Ah dig it too.' Then this grey beard guy whacks his arm around Clayton, squeezes him an sez, 'Hey gubba, you come up too little cuzzy-brud!'

'Yeah yeah,' says Clayton. I haven't a clue what they're on about but they're happy and it's Clayton's shout.

'Somethin from the Spirit. Sometimes we don't wait too long in La Perouse. Just pass. He live here, Spirit – you know?'

'Yeah sure!'

Clayton raps with this guy. Says something about the Devil. The grey bearded guy replies, 'Take all the people – put em under ground. Bad spirit. Bloody dinko spirit, you know.' This is exactly what Clayton wants. This is Clayton-Heaven.

'What's all that about?' I ask Neil.

'Oh, we fixed your mate up with Dreamtime Charlie. He does that spirit talk. No one here'll hear him out, except the Crackers. Not in this pub mate, they're all Aussies.'

'Which one is Clayton - a Honky or a Cracker?'

'Ah,' sighs Neil, 'not now.'

Meanwhile Jay's being shouted a Fossies by the guy on his right while being touched up for a few bob by the guy on his left. Guys are helping themselves to my ciggies, others are offering me free ones. Bob's the clear favourite. They keep calling him *Brudder* and *Cuzzy-Brud.* But it's not all good. In the far corner there's another bunch who keep staring as if they want to deck us. So all in all it's a pretty active scene – or so it seems to me, who's only really ever been to the Greengate and Waitara's Blue Gum Hotel.

Before we even start a blackfella called Harold in an oversized t-shirt asks, 'You sing *Cold Cold Heart?*'

'Not that one,' Mark cuts in, 'but lots of others'.

With Neil's help we eventually find the powerpoint. 'Nearly ready to go?' he asks? Where's Bob?

'Over there.'

'You with the band?' asks a woman with the thickest lips I've ever seen.

I reply, 'Yeah,'

'I'm Hazel…' and before I get to say anything else, she grabs me by the back of the neck and pulls my mouth hard against hers. She forces my lips apart and I'm shocked, disgusted and scared – raising my eyes to the guys in the corner who don't seem to like it. As the kiss goes on, I realise just how much nicer these thick soft lips are compared to whitegirl lips. *This* is a real mouth. A Thunderbird with fins!

'You sing *Cold Cold Heart?'*

'Um...' I pull away from Hazel a bit more reluctantly than I expected when this started.

'Cos I can sing it if you want?'

'Well, that's great mate,' I tell him. 'I'll remember that later'.

Back to business - plug in, find my plectrum, order stage beers, test the mike, tune up.

'What did the sheep say to the shearer?' I speak into the mike. 'Ewe-calyptus - testing testing. *Ah look at ewe with your sad dark eyes* - testing one-two-three. How's that?'

Neil fiddles with a few dials and says, 'Go again...' which I do. Then - adjustments. Retune. Drum roll. Applause.

'Where'ya from?' someone yells at Bob. 'I ain seen you round Redfern!'

'Mum came from Alice...'

'Alice Spring way?' says someone else, pointing to a woman, 'She from Alice!' but the Alice woman don't look up.

And so we begin. Thrash thrash thrash – best song, *My Generation.* Hoots and whistles when it ends.

'What you wanna die for?' someone yells out, 'when you get old.'

'Cos I wanna stay young and different!' I reply.

'You already pretty different!' someone else mocks, chucking a beer can. I duck. Everyone finds that funny.

'C'mon Mark – quick, *For Your Love!'*

We play it. Five people clap.

'Play something by the Kinks or the Manfreds...' I tell the band, a bit desperately, '...something with a beat!' 'Play *Cold Cold Heart!'*

'Yeah!' Everyone starts yelling for *Cold Cold Heart.*

I start figuring out its three chords and try to remember the words so I can sing it. Mark follows me on bass but Jay puts down his instrument an wanders off. Then Harold shoves me aside and starts singing. He sings awful, too close to the mike. They LOVE im!

Huge enormous cheer! Whistles! More! More!

'Ya kno *Liddle Boy Loss?'* continues Harold. Ashamed as I am to admit it, I do know the chords. I start strumming oom-chick oom-chick oom-chick and away he goes, '*In the wile Noo England Ranges…*'. Cheers! Whistles! Yeah! Yeah! More!

Jay's totally given up on geetar. He calls for a beer and joins Clayton and Dreamtime Charlie. I want im back.

'Here's a little bit of Blues…' I announce, trying to regain the mike. 'This one's called *Baby Please Doan Go* – know it Harold?

'Naaa…'. He scuttles offstage, disappointed cos he wanted to sing the night out.

'Hey Jay! Over here! *Baby Please Doan Go!'*

That one always gets Jay in. He fairly cooks. We burn.

'More Blues!' yells Hazel, who I am thinking about all the time now.

'Okay,' I tell the band, '12-bar in E. I'll make up the words…'

Harold is on vocals
Hazel's kinda nice
Bob is playing on the drums
And (something something) twice
I got them blues boy…

'No way…' says Jay. 'Give it away…'.

'Give it to Bob,' says Mark.

BOB! BOB! So I hand Bob my axe and settle behind the kit that I doan kno how to play, so I tap the snare and clunk the foot pedal on the first beat of every bar. Thump-2-3-4. Thump 2-3-4. It's okay.

Bob takes over the singing, '*There's a game called World War 3 and I think this is it.'* They fucken luv im! Biggest cheer for da Brudder!

‘This is a song I wrote…’ he says, and I have no idea what it is. Some song he carried inside him and never shared with the band.

Never bin reel happy Lord, in this my 16th year…

Mark can’t pick up on it and occasionally thumps Bass E. Jay keeps the chords coming and I hit the snare hard on the first beat of each bar and tap softly for the rest. (*Never hit the cymbals* - that’s what I reckon. Remember that and not much else, and it’s possible to survive behind a kit.)

Next another song I’ve never heard Bob do. *The Drought* – it kills them.

If it don’t rain down south we’ll be ruined
If it don’t rain up north she’ll be worse
If it don’t start rainin soon
You might as well assume
All my farming days will be over.

What happens next I simply don’t believe, cos it works. Bob gets it into his head to sing – oh no – not *Running Bear!* This makes even the mean guys up the back sit up and listen. This is Bob’s audience man. I mean – he’s always been a bit of a star at skool, but never like this. How will we ever get him behind a drumkit again?

On the banks…oompa oompa
Of the river…oompa oompa

Towards the end of the second chorus I see a huge black guy in a red shirt walk up to the stage, mean. He cases us, counting white scalps it seems to me. He gives me the bird, like *fuckyoukid.* But it’s not me he’s after. It’s some guy down the front, dancing, drinking, going oompa-oompa and cheering for more Bob.

The big guy clouds up, takes two steps back. His eyes widen and he launches himself slowly. Just as *Little White Dove is about to dive into the ragin river* he gives a kinda roar, rushes the oompa guy and crushes him against the wall.

Down they go. *Ah, fuck, ggaah* noises. Ker-lang goes the mike stand. They crash into Jay’s amp. Bob is knocked backwards. The drumkit scatters. Glasses hit the floor - smash - and the big guy starts strangling the other bloke who makes *ghahggah* throat noises.

We’re confused, trying to save our equipment. We’re hoping Jay’s amp still works. It mightn’t, it’s a valve amp. Back comes that skoolkid fear that when you’re broke and something’s wrecked, it’s gonna take six months to afford the damage. Meanwhile it’s two hands around this guy’s throat – what’s this, a killing?

Clayton races over. Neil whistles for an even bigger guy, and between them, the three of them pull the fighters apart. I’m scared the whole place is gonna erupt into one big war and we’re nowhere near an exit. Eventually, the two fighters get pulled apart, with the big guy standing and gasping and the other guy on his knees, flicking his eyes wildly around the room as if he's lost something.

'You'll be right mate,' says Neil to the partially strangled guy, bleeding – pro'bly from broken glass. 'Doan get up jess yet…'.

'Cool it Max!' orders Neil to the big guy. 'One more and yer OUT! An I bloody mean ut.' Big Max looks as if he wants to land one more punch – maybe on Neil himself, the oompa-guy or – godnose - maybe me. 'One more and you're out fer good – understand!'

Big Max gets the pitcher and shuffles into the corner back to the mean guys. Neil picks a mike from the floor, tests it, then announces, 'S'all right folks, someone just fell over…'. Turns to us and says, 'Keep playing…!'

'What'll we play?'

'*Catch the Wind* – or something slow.'

That's what we do. *In the chilly airs and minutes of uncertainty…'* oh god.

'Play *Cold Cold Heart!'* yells Harold. And, having decided to go with the flow, that's what we play next. Harold hops up to the mike and sings it it again. YAY!

We also play *Pub With No Beer* with three different vocalists, *Rock Around the Clock,* twice. *Crying* by Roy Orbison with Hazel on vocals. Then, *Little Boy Lost, Save the Last Dance for Me, Royal Telephone, Only the Lonely* and a Buddy Williams song about beer that I don't really follow.

We're welcomed back 'any time'. Get paid $10 each. Neil says *Communist Girls* was pretty good and that he could introduce us to a guy called Brian Vogue who runs Linda Lee Records. Three girls hang around Bob the whole time we're packing up.

Hazel wetly kisses me goodbye.

And Harold reckons we're the best band he's ever heard and we can back him any time.

As we leave, we hear Neil whooping it up on blues harp, with the whole place stamping and cheering and stomping.

18

The Loved One

We're at Jay's place. Just him and me. Sucking beers in his bedroom, where he now keeps his motorbike beside his bed. 'You miss Stu?' I ask.

'Yeah sure,' he replies, 'Stu was a good bent guy to drink with. It's a special talent that he had'.

'Oh yeah! Like calling Tony a "Wog" and getting into that blue with Bob!'

'Naah, he wasn't like that all the time. Just that he gets a bit agro around skoolies...tries to freak em out or somethin.'

'What was the verdict?'

'He got off with a two year bond. But a condition was that he goes back to Melbourne and lives at home. Hard luck though, in court...'

'Whaddya mean?'

'There was four of them involved and they said Stu was the ringleader. Shane was too drugfucked to know what was going on, another guy was under 16 and the other guy, well...I guess he had a good lawyer.'

'Still, a 24-month bond and he's not in the pen.'

'Oh he was for a bit...'

'What happened?'

'Well, the rich kid – the one with the lawyer – knew of a house in Wahroonga that they could break into. And Shane knew how to shift the stuff after. So they did it. Shane stayed in the car.'

'How's they catch Stu?'

'Shane's friends just set im up and pissed off.'

'Is she all right?'

'She's either in women's prison or in Wisteria House, drying out. I can give you Stu's number if you want...'.

'I doan want to phone Stu.'

'Why not?'

'He's a thief, a shoplifter, starts fights, calls people *Wogs* and hates music...' I say, opening another beer, 'he wasted your time really.'

'Well, Stu never did like that longhair stuff.'

'That's so weird,' I reckon, 'First thing I'll do when I leave home is grow my hair, but he never grew his. I'll grow mine to my shoulders!'

'Me too...'

'What's it all about Jay? Five months from the end of the skool year - hopefully uni for me. Also I think we've got to register for the ballot, which is one reason I've really *got* to get into uni, to get a deferral from Military Service.'

'Well, I'd like to do something with my music,' Jay strums as he talks, 'I listen to bluesmen – BB King, John Lee Hooker, Lightning Hopkins, ah drink a few beers, pull out the guitar and copy their licks. The thing with musical instruments is the more you play them, the more you learn. I've got my whole life ahead of me, there's no need to rush. I'm buying a Wah-Wah Pedal next.'

'What about marriage?'

'Everybody else gets married, I s'pose I will too. Can't do nuthin bout that – kids, home, you know…it just *happens* I guess. And it all starts with a girlfriend.'

'Girlfriends are a hassle,' I reply.

'Why?'

'They push you around.'

'They doan push me around. Neither does my Mum. You doan have to let people do it to you. You've actually got a choice in this…'.

'But you've left skool!'

'Oh sure, but no one pushes me around at work. And when I was at skool I got away with a lot more than you do. I didn't draw attention to myself. Also I made it difficult for them to discipline me.'

'It's not like that Jay. It's like – when I walk into a pub, up the Cross, or somewhere like that – I feel like a grown-up. But at skool, I'm still a kid. On weekends I have all these experiences, and then Monday it's back to regulation socks and getting yelled at for talkin. I mean, talking is what we're doing now, yet at skool you get yelled at for doin it. Or you have to write *I must not talk in class* 100 times as punishment. That is a real weird thing to happen to anyone, having to spend their time writing *I must not talk in class* on four exercise book-size pages. Isn't that weird at 18?'

'You're not listening mate…'

'I am listening, just not believing I have a choice in this if I want to avoid Military Service.'

'Nothing terrible happens when you say no. Just say *NO, I'm not cutting my hair,* what can they do? Expel you – right? That won't kill you. Jess just go to another skool or tech or somethin. You can do it. The teacher's have got you bluffed. Outside those skool gates, they've got no hold on you whatever. I've got a real job mate. When the foreman comes up to us guys in the print shop, he's got to watch himself. The guys I work with don't naturally go *yes sir, no sir.* They might say *fuck off prick* if they doan like what he's on about. And if he carries on too much, we walk off the job. That's how we deal with bosses. An that's what you've got to learn if you want people to take you seriously. That's why Stu always took the piss out of you, all that skooly shit.'

'Okay, okay – what else is new? Did you see our graffiti?'

'What graffiti?' Jay smiles.

'In the concrete, outside Mark's place.'

'What's it say?'

'Just our names. Clayton wrote CS, Mark wrote *Sonic* and I wrote Tom with an exclamation mark an all.'

'Oh, you mean cement graffiti? Hey – who's Elton Bottom? There's Elton Bottom written in the concrete at the place you're pro'bably talkin about.'

'Oh... Ellen Bolton! She goes to Hornsby Girls High.'

'Mind if I strum while you talk?'

'Go fer it, I'm jess thinking about what you said about saying NO. Something's got to click in your head I suppose, and then after you've said it once, it might be hard to ever say YES again'.

19

Go Now

Paul McCartney has admitted to dropping acid. It's all the news. That and the 6-Day War. We've now got postcodes and STD phones. That's big news too. Postcodes are based on military zonings, so I have an argument with Devlin about postcodes being code for 'war'. But the biggest news in the whole world is that Paul McCartney has dropped acid. So has Billy Thorpe.

Something's happening. The generations are getting scareder of each other. *The Trip* by Donovan is banned. *Puff the Magic Dragon* is kinda banned. The Boss smashed Bob's *Sgt Peppers* in front of the skool assembly as an 'example' to us all. How does that make sense? The Anti-Vietnam marches are getting angrier. I'm beginning to hate things I used to only dislike. My jeans are more torn and staying that way. My hair is longer than usual. I don't shave more than I have to. The Boss sent for me the other day. I knew it was about hair or wearing rings or some stupid bloody thing so I didn't go. *Didn't get the message*, I said when he caught up with me. Next day, I wagged it. I went to Jay's garage instead of attending skool. He took a sickie from work and we spent the day playing guitar and knocking back tubes. I've not been like that before. I get headaches.

Sunday arvos I usually take Salli to *Beethoven's Disco* near Central. Watch Jeff St John & Yama. The keyboard player is Groove Myers and we like him doing Chuck Berry's *It Goes to Show You Never Can Tell.* I dance so close to the amps that my ears whistle for half hour afterwards. I do it all the time.

No one in my class gives a shit about *The Blitz.* While the Mob are heroes at their skool, I feel like an embarrassment at ours.

I'm sitting on the verandah eating a sandwich with John Vote Pye. John threatened to give me lines the other day for 'flaunting' some rule. He reckons he can't really overlook things like that, so we talk it through, even though he swears he got to be a prefect without my help. But he agrees it'd be wrong to give lines to a mate. I tell him skool rules, like all rules, are a figment of someone's desire to push people around. There is no right and wrong in long or short hair, red or grey socks. Just Grey Sox Verses NOT Grey Sox. The question is *which side are you on Pye?* Theirs or ours? 'I'm with youse guys,' he replies.

Devlin walks past, 'Pick up that piece of paper! Straighten your ties!' And walks off.

Bearing an armful of skoolbooks, Janet joins us. She's a 'good girl'. I'm wondering whether it's all bin worth it to her - being perfect to become a prefect. When people ask how I spent my 1967, at least I'm spared the embarrassment of saying, 'I spent 1967 being a prefect'.

'Everything's going bad...' I tell Janet, as John sticks his sandwich wrapping in the bin and leaves us to ourselves.

'What do you mean?'

'Everything really. Skool.'

'What's wrong with it?'

'I doan know. I used to feel just *naughty* when I was out of uniform in junior skool, and maybe I thought the teachers had a right to put me through all that shit. I doan feel that way any more, I now think *how dare they!* See – Clayton and Jay have both got jobs, an I hear what they're talkin about and it's not kids stuff. They're both exactly my age. They've got their own dough. No one frisks them for cigs. No one freaks if they grow sidelevers. They wear coloured socks to work. It's difficult to explain that I'm late for band practice because of an after-skool detention. They really don't get it.'

'If socks are so unimportant…' she says, '…avoid the hassle and wear the grey ones, what difference does it make?'

'That's *exactly* my point. If socks are so unimportant, who fucken cares? Pardon the French, Janet.'

Mark flashes past, 'Band practice Sat'dy?'

'Yup.'

Back to Janet, she asks, 'How's Stu?'

'Got a two year bond.'

'How'd he get caught?'

'They'd gotten rid of the stuff before the cops showed up at Shane's, but in the flat was a PJ Proby single with the owner's actual name handwritten on the label. That was the evidence. Shane's in worse trouble, maybe.'

'Who's Shane?'

Big sigh, 'Some other time…'.

Time to move on. I go see Kennedy who is teaching the Colour Wheel to third form. When he sees me, he gets them painting, comes over and talks. Doesn't say, 'Straighten your tie, get those stupid rings off your finger, you're hair's growing a bit, show me your socks'. None of that. Just hi.

Hello Mr Kennedy.

'Not…ah…kicked out of class again Tom?'

'No…ha ha ha, not yet!'

'Oh good, I'm glad you came - because I've got some awful news and I want to share it with someone who might understand.'

'Shoot…'

'He hasn't died yet, but Magritte…' he doesn't finish the sentence.

I try hard to remember what Kennedy taught us about Magritte. He's the guy with the bowler hats and clouds. I think he's got something to do with de

Chirico, Dalí and Man Ray. Ker-yst, why don't I pay attention in Art class? I've got to wing this conversation.

'Is he in a bad way or something?'

'He's not going to make it, that's what they're saying…'.

'Magritte heh?' I reply as thoughtfully as I can manage.

'It'll be sad if he dies Tom.'

'Oh yeah, terrible. Terrible. I've bin thinking about Art lately. Not so much Magritte, but I did chase down some of those other artists. I saw a picture of Andy Warhol's *Triple Elvis*.

'What did you make of it?'

'Loved it.' I notice on his desk a book he's reading.

He says, 'Oh that…it's that book I was telling you about, *Portrait of Vincent* by Hanson. I…ah…read it through each year.'

"Dies at the end, I guess…' I shrug. Stupid thing to say. Everyone dies at the end of a biography. 'Doesn't he cut his ear off then kill himself?'

'Oh, it's terrible when that happens. I always have a bit of a weep when he shoots himself. Then he doesn't die. His friend…ah…Dr Gachet tries to save him. Sends for Theo. Then Vincent loses the will to live and that's it'.

'What happens to Theo?'

'He collapsed at the...ah...graveside, returned to Paris and died shortly afterwards. The two are buried side-by-side. I've got a photo of their gravestones somewhere.'

'I wish you could hear our band Mr Kennedy. We're better now. We've covered a lot of ground, honest. We're even talking about cutting a single. I should tape it for you on the reel-to-reel?'

'You know I'm not crazy about…ah…Rock'.

'But you've gotta like the Beatles! Even Mum likes one or two of their songs…?'

'Some of their melodies aren't too bad. That Bob Dylan is more interesting. He's got a terrible voice but some of his words are pretty good. *It's Alright Ma, I'm Only…ah…Bleedin.* Ah heard that one the other day.'

'Have you heard Gerry Humphries of the Loved Ones?'

'I only really listen to jazz – Dave Brubeck, Charlie Parker, Mingus, Miles…ah…Davies. Thelonius Monk, Sonny Stitt. Any of those ring a bell?'

'Well, Dave Brubeck had a hit called *Take Five.* But John Lennon hates jazz…'.

'Maybe you should think a bit...er...for yourself...' and he quickly slips back into his class and tell a couple of girls to settle down. Then back to me: 'Yes jazz! I like it because of the ah colours in the music itself. Wonderful, wonderful abstract forms – like a musical Jackson Pollock picture. I listen to jazz to ah…lift me. That's what I always play in my studio at home when I ah…paint'.

'Mr Kennedy, does that make you happy?'

'I'm as happy, I er suppose, as a man can be in this life. Sometimes I'm *really* happy when I'm in the middle of a painting, when I reach the point where I can see the end from the beginning. That's happy. But whenever I get too content…something comes along and bowls me sideways. Like Magritte being seriously ill. I really care about my er heroes. How bout you?'

'I'm happy when it's all going well in front of an audience. There's an incredible thing about an audience that's excitement-plus!'

And there goes the bell.

*

I head for the library, and what do I see when I walk in, but my whole class – prefects n all – piled up on the main table – singing.

Singing?

The Skool Concert's coming up - that must be it. Everyone is stacked all over each other, on the table, looking down at the one sheet of music that Jenny owns an most of them can't see. They're all singin *Green Green Grass of Home.* All of them – Colin, Peter, Ian, Daks, Pye, Mark, Janet, Jenny, Sue, Janine, Geoff, Andrew, Adrian - more. It looks like a monkey tree, so I climb on top of the pile and sing green green grass of home too. *And they'll all come to see me…smiling sweetly…* an all that. Big voice. Ha ha ha goes everyone, what about *Everglades? Running like a dog through the slimy bog…*

They all go, good song! I go oops nearly lost my balance. This is dumb and I'm dumbing along with everything. Skitas. Gaters, Wrong socks. Sidelevers. Skool Concert.

Piled up, I'm crushing Jenny. 'Shog off Tom!' That's her quoting *Henry V Act 2.*

In walks Hopkins, the youngest staff member, not even 21. And us 18. He's expected to punish people my age. Thanks to the Wyndham Scheme, he's an adult and we're still bloody kids.

Hopkins isn't a mean guy. A bit like John really – someone handed him a badge. I know Hopkins from the Chess Club. I thrash him like I thrash everyone else. But whipping Hopkins at Chess isn't much of a claim. Even first formers do that. And he's pretty good about it too. 'Congratulations!' he always exclaims, shaking hands with some 14-year old. But Hopkins has no discipline. Can't hold a class together. Being teacherly seems to freak him out a bit. One time Hopkins walked into a junior class where a kid had his back to him. He said 'turn around' and the entire class turned itself around. Stuff like that happens to him all the time. Hopkins is a wimp but a good un.

Today, he sees us all piled up – singin. These are prefects, skool captains, sixth formers, caught in a silly moment. He should have waited for us to unravel – what else are we gonna do? Nuthin. What's Jenny gonna do? Janet? And Adrian? Now that a teacher's walked in they're obviously gonna to stop.

Instead, Hopkins panics and starts yellin, 'This is a disgrace sixth form! I've never seen such a sight in the library before!'

I've seen a better one.

Last week I spotted Johnny McMasters giving Karen Boyle a right feel-up in the Reference Section.

'Tom Truscott! Get out!' he yells, forgetting that in the past he's treated me like a bit of a friend. Meanwhile the rest sort themselves out. Everyone shuts up and sits themselves around the long library tables. Everything's back to where it should be. The good girls are back to being good. The sports hero is remembering his bloody responsibilities. But Hawkins has told me to get out.

I'm expecting him to take it back and I say, 'Hang about mate, everything's back to normal'.

'OUT!' he explodes, red-faced and stupid.

And then I say, 'NO'.

We've certainly captured everyone's attention. Hopkins doesn't know what to do next.

'I told you to leave, now go.'

'Why?'

'Don't argue!'

'Don't argue? Since when did that ever make sense…!'

'Get out.'

'But EVERYONE was involved in this.'

'You were the ringleader!' he snaps.

'He wasn't!' says Jenny. I would have thought her authority as Skool Captain might have counted for something.

'Tom was NOT the ringleader!' Peter Prefect joins in. Peter? (I always thought he had it in for me. Here he is sticking up for me.)

John won't be left out, 'That's right, he wasn't!'

It's all too much for Hopkins, everyone calling out like that. Now it's Mark, 'Tom only arrived half a minute before you did!'

Totally confused, Hopkins turns to me and reiterates, 'O-U-T spells out.'

'What is this? Remedial Spelling or something…?'

Everyone laughs. Now I feel guilty for poking fun. Okay, I'll go.

'Don't go!' This is Peter again.

'Yeah, Tom's in the right for once!'

'Don't go Tom,' says John, 'siddown'.

That's exactly what I do.

'Please leave...' says Hopkins, realizing we're now in freefall, 'You have to obey me, I'm a teacher'.

The person who leaves the room isn't me, but Hopkins.

Two minutes later he comes back with Mr Ingles, Head of the Science Department.

'Tom Truscott!' he orders, 'You've been told to get out, now GET OUT!' God, he's loud. Chucks a bigger tantrum than my little sister.

'Ferget it Tom,' John again.

'How *dare* you,' Ingles snaps at John, 'A prefect! Adopting that tone!'

Hopkins slinks against the wall.

Then Ingles turns back to me, 'I'm saying this just once more Tom – leave now'.

'NO.'

Hopkins and Ingles walk out together. The next person through the door is Calder, playing Deputy I suppose - not in the role of Ancient History teacher, that's fer sure. To the rest of the class he says, 'The rest of you...get on with your work, I don't want to hear a sound'. Then he looks me up and down like I'm crazy or something and says, 'Now you Tom - the boy who'll only take orders when they suit him!'

'But it wasn't *fair* Mr Calder!'

'It wasn't *unfair* either. You were simply asked to leave the room while Mr Hopkins restored order. You'd be back inside as soon as he straightened everything out, you know that.'

'The point is Mr Calder, all teachers see me and see red'.

'That's not right,' Calder continues, 'Skool is a system. In order for any system to work effectively it needs a chain of command. I see in you a boy who may excel at Art and Ancient History if only we can keep him here long enough to sit his HSC. I see a boy who has one last chance to walk out that door. Even then in may be too late...'

'Whaddya mean *too late?*'

'When it comes to insubordination, the school has no choice. If you won't obey orders, the school can't keep you.'

'I'm sorry Mr Calder, it's no big deal and I'm staying put.' Exit Calder.

Suddenly the library door is flung open crash and in walks the Boss and he towers over me, 'How dare you question one of my teachers you disreputable long-haired lout! Go to my office Thomas Truscott, I've already discussed the matter with your parents!'

'But...'

‘You have no case! Look at you! And where’s that other one?’ He scours the room til his eyes land on Mark. ‘You boy, are forbidden to attend any more classes until you get a decent haircut’. Mark appears shocked. ‘You can sit in the Assembly Hall until you cut that hair!’ Then back to me.

‘GO NOW!’

I pack up and go. But I didn’t lose outright. I drove three of them crazy. That was something.

As I leave the library I bump into Hopkins, really distraught, telling me he’s so sorry the whole thing blew up the way it did.

I wish he’d thought of that 20 minutes ago.

*

In the evening the Boss comes to our house, sits on the nite n day and talks to my oldies.

Verdict: I am suspended for a fortnight for ‘insubordination’ and John Pye has been suspended for one week for egging me on.

Egging me on!

Dad says he will support the skool in its decision. And from his end, I will be grounded for the whole fortnight, to feel the full weight of punishment.

‘I want Thomas to understand, that this is the harshest penalty we could impose, short of expulsion…’ the bald-headed Boss continues, ‘…which he escaped because Mr Kennedy, Mr Calder and Mr Hopkins spoke in favour of retaining him’.

He drones on. Slaghead bastard. He uses words like attitude, haircut, waste of talent, lack of application, not fitting in, unhealthy interest in the opposite sex, no sense of decency, bad influence on juniors, lack of concentration, too much Rock N Roll and no proper sports uniform.

Dad mostly back-peddles, dropping his real estate business into the conversation only occasionally, just to remind the Boss I do have another option if necessary. Weirdly, when the Boss gets to mentioning Mark and the Blitz, Dad sticks up for me.

‘I don’t care a fig for that sort of music,’ says Dad, ‘But I am pleased to see their entrepreneurial spirit. They performed somewhere near Redfern and Tom came home with a $10 bill’. The Boss won’t ever win, talking to Dad about money.

Instead, the Boss starts saying about what bands ‘do’. In his roundabout way he reminds Dad they take drugs and screw girls. Oh, bands are nuthin to do with music. Taking drugs and screwing girls is all he knows about bands, the bugger.

‘I don’t think my son would take marijuana,’ says Dad, which surprises me.

‘How can you be sure about that?’

'Have you any reason to suggest Tom might be taking drugs?'

'Not specifically, no.'

'Tom?' asks my father, 'Have you been smoking marijuana?'

'I've never smoked marijuana in my life,' I reply truthfully.

Not long afterwards Dad walks the Boss to the front door.

'Very good of you to take this trouble after hours,' says Dad. Big sincere handshake between the men and promises they'll cooperate with each other to make a decent citizen out of me.

How can a good semi-religious couple, with a flourishing real estate business on Sydney's north shore come up with a hopeless son like me? Mum and Dad are wondering the same thing. I can see that the Boss considers my father to be a very decent citizen. It's just his bloody son that no one can explain.

My ole man closes the door. We hear the sound of the Boss turning his motor over before driving off. With a bit of luck, maybe he'll kill himself on the roads.

Dad walks back into the lounge room, heaves a big sigh. It's his duty, I guess to give me a bloody big lecture. Mum expects it. Instead, he sits in his armchair, lights up a smoke, switches on the telly and flicks through the book he is currently reading while the telly warms up. He's reading *Afternoon Light* by Sir Robert Menzies.

My ole man looks at me out of the corner of his eye and turns up the volume. We watch *The Fugitive* together without either of us saying a word.

20

Tired of Trying, Sick of Lying, Scared of Lying

Mark and Samantha have heaps of sex. On Saturday afternoons, Clayton, Jay and Bob drop by Mark's flat, as did I before getting grounded, an everyone plays 500 while they lie in bed. Nowadays, Mark and Samantha hardly get out of bed. No one smokes in the bedroom.

Samantha still reckons she knows what's hip and uphip. She a hippo-maniac. Maybe she's right. Maybe it's no longer the Who and the Yardbirds? Maybe it's the time of Jefferson Airplane and the Grateful Dead.

I can't believe it! Why not the Who? – the best band in the history of Planet Earth? And here's this American-Aussie chick who sez Daddy telling me that everything I believed about smashing guitars is old and being up-to-date means wearing flowers and kissing everyone hello. But I don't want to be *nice.*

Even so, Samantha always reckons she knows best. She's traveled and I ain't. She says we should blitz our parents and teachers out with luv.

Imagine me coming through the front door, 'Hi Mum, I love you!' If I said *I love you* and handed her a bunch of flowers, she'd definitely think I was on drugs.

Indifference is something you can trust. Love is more complicated.

Samantha hates all Aussie bands. She reckons Gerry Humphries is nothing but a screecher. The Easybeats aren't artistic enough. And the Missing Links are disgusting punks. Luv, she says, is all you need. Samantha has taken to saying she 'loves' me. She says it in a smarmy tone. Well, I still bloody hate her.

Well...I don't really, not quite. In fact we've bin gettin on okay recently.

But I'm grounded now.

I'm not allowed out of the suburb. The furthest I can go is to Salli's place where I listen to the *Animalisms* LP. Or up the road to Mark's place and hang there. Not even allowed to catch a train to Jay's place in Gordon, but I do anyway.

Dad's first thought was to pull me out of private skool and send me straight to St Ives High. I didn't care one way or the other. Then, after three days he changed his mind and reckoned that I should finish what I started.

At home I work my arse off on a mammoth Ancient History assignment about the Peloponnesian War, but I do no other skoolwerk, cept Art, where I find out that Magritte painted an amazing picture called *The Lost Jockey.*

Then, I see it in the papers - Magritte dies, 15 August.

In my bedroom, I write poems and songs, and invent characters like Little Jenny Puffin and Lord Casey Garfunkel, for stories that never get written.

I read some of my poems to Bob who says yeah, they're okay. I suggest he set a couple more to music and he picks on one called *Nuthin.*

Yeah, I work some more on the Peloponnesian War and get some books on the subject from Hornsby Library. Dad takes me to his office where I work half a day until I get bored filing real estate ads. He kicks me out. Says I'm an embarrassment. We argue about my hair and I catch the train home. Back home I write a poem called *Nude Swimmer.*

Then I do a picture full of Egyptian-type images and Samantha names it *Egyptian Kaleidoscope,* because she says *Kaleidoscope* is a hot word. I start sketching my friends.

I do a really good one of Salli, which I give her for her birthday. And a crook one of Mark that he chucks in the bin. I also draw a band symbol for the Blitz, which everyone reckons looks a bit too similar to a swastika.

Salli drops in and tells me Woody Guthrie is on the ropes with a rare disease called Huntington's Chorea. She managed to borrow a Woody record and we give it a spin. He sounds a lot like Bob Dylan. She says it's real sad about Woody because he's so wrecked that he doesn't recognize his own songs any more. Plus he's real famous, though he doesn't know what famous is any more.

I go to the St Ives Record Shop and buy *In-A-Gadda-Vida* by Iron Butterfly.

This turns out to be the first Rock record my Dad says he likes. Well, not 'likes'. More that he thinks the band is pretty good on their instruments.

Then we play Chess together as usual and watch TV. The Seekers are on. I really hate them. I'm getting bored and wonder what could possibly happen if I simply stood up and announced, 'I'm going to the Cross tonight with Clayton…!'

Then.

Suddenly.

I glance at the screen and see the Beatles dressed like Hippies, with a small group of pop stars grouped around them - Marianne Faithful, Mick Jagger, Donovan, Jane Asher…

John Lennon is sitting on a stool and singing the biggest broadcast in the history of television, *All You Need is Love.* This really is a big deal. No sex, no drugs, no violence, no cock-rock - all you need is just love, just like Samantha reckons. I don't believe what I'm seeing. John is singing in an ordinary sincere voice while Mum hands me a plate of fish n chips.

Even my parents go hmmm, this changes the face of protest.

We argue afterwards, but not angrily. Somehow we've all been slightly affected by this uncomplicated message. Clayton's been saying it for ages. My father says it's a nice ideal, but would it work? Is all you need love? Even I disagree a bit. Sometimes I think all you need is justice.

I get the picture. We have to be kinder to each other if we want to make a decent go of our lives. We have to be gentler with our parents and maybe they in turn will treat us properly.

It's up to my generation to clean up the mess the previous generation made. It's up to us to end the racism and the wars. It's all up to us. I want to become a vegetarian. I wanna quit the cigs and smoke peppermint tea instead. *All you need is luv.*

Mum tries to swat a blowfly.

I say, 'Don't do that, it might have family and kids'.

My parents look rather startled.

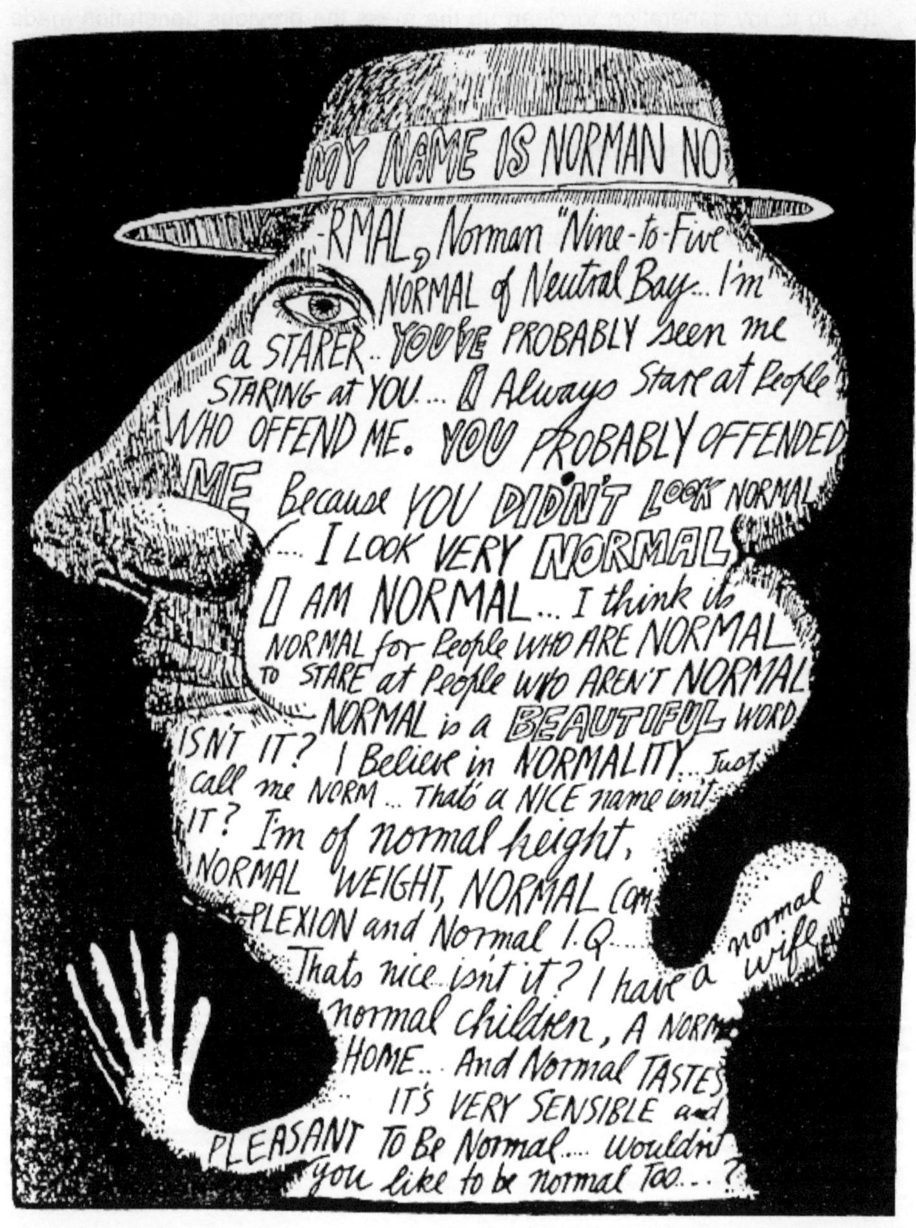
MY NAME IS NORMAN NO
-RMAL, Norman "Nine-to-Five
NORMAL of Neutral Bay... I'm
a STARER.. YOU'VE PROBABLY seen me
STARING at YOU.... I Always Stare at People
WHO OFFEND ME. YOU PROBABLY OFFENDED
ME Because YOU DIDN'T LOOK NORMAL
.... I LOOK VERY NORMAL
I AM NORMAL... I think it's
NORMAL for People WHO ARE NORMAL
TO STARE at People who AREN'T NORMAL
NORMAL is a BEAUTIFUL WORD
ISN'T IT? I Believe in NORMALITY... Just
call me NORM... That's a NICE name isn't
IT? I'm of normal height,
NORMAL WEIGHT, NORMAL COM-
PLEXION and Normal I.Q....
That's nice isn't it? I have a normal wife
normal children, A NORM
HOME... And Normal TASTES
... IT'S VERY SENSIBLE and
PLEASANT TO Be Normal.... Wouldn't
you like to be normal Too...?

21

My Pink Half of the Drainpipe

I have a dream.

I have a dream that I am ordinary, sensible and a stockbroker.

The lawn is mowed on Sundays.

My wife has a second car.

My children are a pigeon pair.

I wear Fletcher Jones trousers and Julius Marlow shoes.

Everywhere I go people comment on what a stable influence I am, how mature.

I talk more about sport than I do Art.

I talk about the balance of payments figure more than I talk about injustice.

My parents, my former schoolchums, my colleagues, all applaud me as the well-centred person that I am.

'That Tom really knows how to discipline his kids!' I hear them proudly announce as I thrash my teenage son for underachieving. 'That Tom is to be admired!'

I also dream that I die at 42 without a cause.

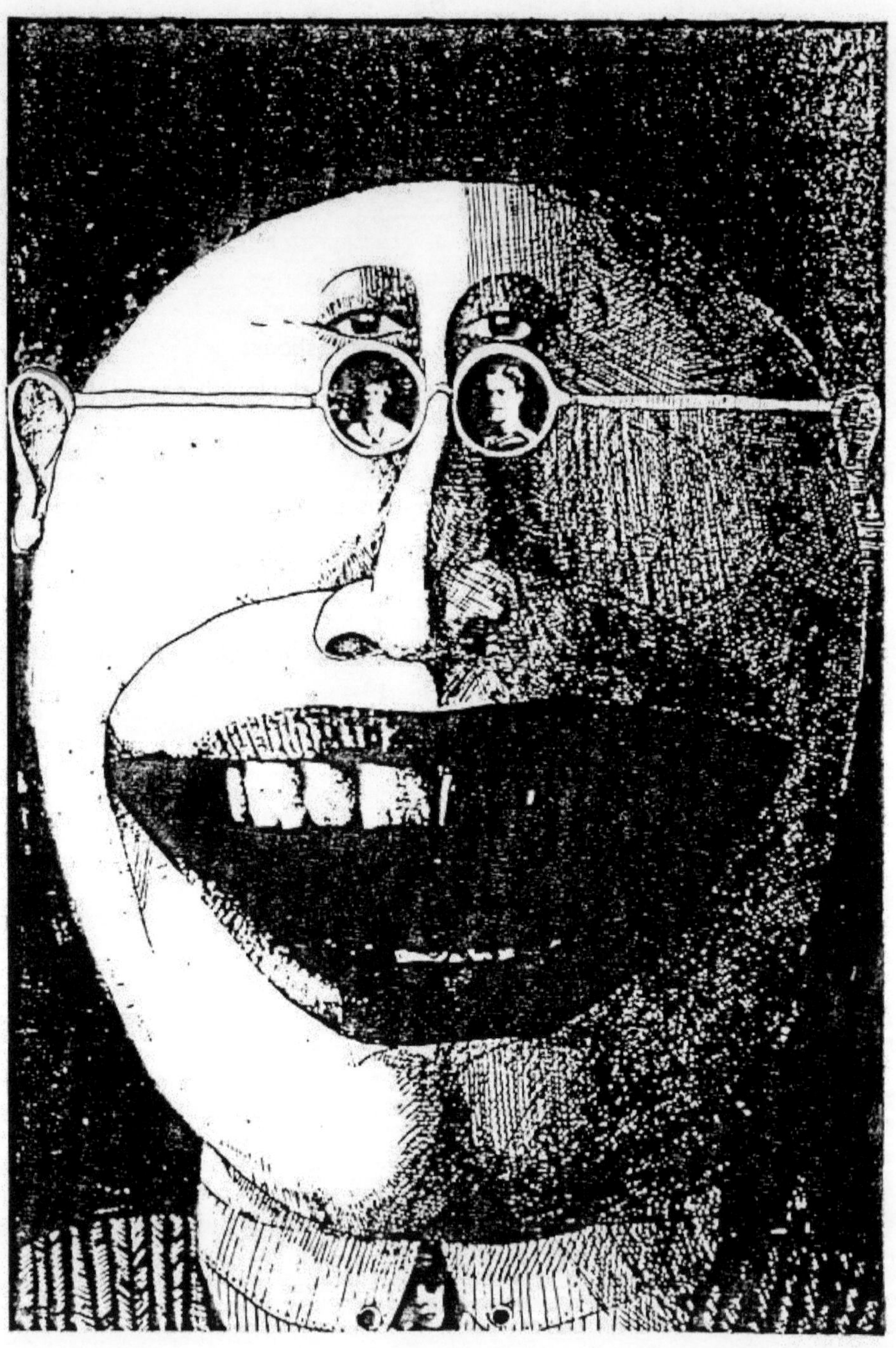

22

Manic Depression

I have a dream.

There is a room as big as the world and as old as time. In this room everyone has a turn.

Colin had his and he forgave everybody.

Adrian had his turn and reckoned the world was fair.

John has had his and said, it could've been better but he doesn't have any serious complaints.

Jenny has had hers and told everyone they were great.

And I am waiting for my chance.

It is the Universal Courtroom. Every girl I've ever known is there. My parents and their parents are there. Cousin Ken has a full metal jacket. The Blitz are holding their instruments. The scene is the cover of *Sgt Peppers*-cum-Day of Judgement.

Allen Ginsberg, Bob Dylan, Mary Quant, Woody Guthrie, Howlin Wolf, Marianne Faithful, Paul McCartney, Agent 99, Mick Jagger, Donovan, Syd Barrett, John Lennon, Janis Joplin, Ringo, Gerry Humphries, Karen Dalton, Viv Stanshall, Phil May, Bridget Riley, Yoko Ono, Marcel Duchamp, Keith Relf, Ginger Baker, Steve Winwood, Ray Charles, Monet, Jackson Pollock, Martin Sharp, Max Weber, Juliette Greco, Pete Townshend, Snoopy, Ingrid Bergmann, Jim Morrison, Tommy Steele, Marlon Brando, Emily Bronte, Charles Dickens, Andy Warhol, Sam Cooke, Stevie Wright, Bobby & Laurie, Jeff St John, Billy Thorpe, Dinah Lee, Salvadore Dalí, Nina Simone, Jeff Beck, Daphne Du Maurier, Paul Jones, Stuart Sutcliffe, Mike Bloomfield, Tintin, Paul Butterfield, Mahalia Jackson, John Lee Hooker, Martin Luther King, George, Keith Richards, Brian Jones, Vince Melouney, Eric Burdon, Morticia Addams, Batman, Ray Davies, Lolita, Edith Piaf, the Mothers of Invention are there.

Shane is there. Bob is right next to me. Clayton is carrying *On The Road* by Kerouac. Salli is holding an oval mirror. Stu is carrying a flick-knife.

Napoleon Bonaparte, Mickey Mouse, Cleopatra, Madame Defarge, Julius Caesar, Catherine Earnshaw, Edward Lear, Prince Charles, Che Guevara, Rupert Bear, Fidel Castro, Charles De Gaulle, Marie Antoinette, Marie Curie, Long John Silver, Menzies, Beethoven, the Lone Ranger, Phar Lap, Chicester. Every friend I've ever had, everyone who's ever touched me or told me anything is there. Everyone in the whole world is there. God is there.

And I'm next.

Waiting for my turn to be the judge.

God is referee. He is floating above it all like an Indian Mekon, a blue god with many arms. With him, onboard his tiny flying saucer is Ravi Shankar, God's chosen musician.

The angels are all watching, grouped like a footy crowd at the Footy Grand Final.

All the saints, the special people of God are there too – Vincent, James Dean, Rasputin, Magritte, Joan of Arc by George Bernard Shaw, Robin Hood, Maid Marion, Barbarella, Gandhi, Eleanor Rigby. With them are those who have starved and suffered since the dawn of time, the coming of the Rainbow Serpant.

Little Richard is God's chosen choirmaster. Yuri Gagarin, his adviser. Arethra Franklin, his singer. And Jimi, his lead musician. God asks him to play at every opportunity. He loves watching Jimi play the upside-down Strat with his teeth. He is astounded at his own creation!

Brigitte Bardot, of course is Eve. (*And God Created Woman…)*

There is, of course, an entire section dedicated to Marilyn.

The Hunchback of Notre Dame pulls my arm, 'Next!' I walk out into the presence of everyone and everything that has ever existed. It's my turn to judge.

The rules are extremely fair. No one who's been a judge in earth-time gets to judge now. You only ever have one turn. The teachers, parents and the systemites had theirs back then. Now it's ours.

'Your mother!' roars a heavenly voice.

She steps forward. The little lady who married the man who went to war, who had me and my little sis when he came back. Who suckled me as a baby, spanked me when I was bad. Was patient and impatient with me.

'What crimes has she committed against you?' asks the Heavenly Voice.

'Her only real crime, O Lord,' I reply most reverently, 'is that she never liked the Beatles'.

The audience is shocked!

'And how must she be punished?'

'When the British Empire collapsed O Lord, and destroyed all her dreams, she was punished enough. And then came Depression and war. Her husband was sent to New Guinea and she never thought she'd see him again- and she was punished. She was punished when Little Richard sang a crazed version of *Long Tall Sally.* She was punished when the Bodgies and the Widgies hit town. She was punished by the Surfers, Sharpies, Mods and Rockers. She was punished when Menzies was no longer Prime Minister. She was punished by the 60s. She was punished when we grew our hair. She was punished when I got suspended from school. But more than that, she was punished when her father died. O Lord, can we reward my mother? Can we give her the most precious object in the history of the Earth?'

'Of course,' says God, with infinite wisdom. And a small archangel dashes about confused, eventually returning with the deeds to a waterfront block of land in Mosman, and kneels before the Big Blue God.

'No no no!' says the Lord. 'I said the most *precious* object in the entire universe!'

This time the archangel gets it right and we gasp as the archangel hands Mum the painting *Sunflowers* by Vincent.

'Thanks,' she responds merrily, 'I'll hang it in the lounge room above the nite n day'.

'No worries mum,' I give her two thumbs up.

A shadow falls, a dice is cast, cold air fills the Eternity Room.

'Mr Devlin!' roars a voice, 'Your teacher from when you were in Form One. The bastard who caned you maliciously at every opportunity, who humiliated you in front of the girls, who made you cut your hair embarrassingly short. This teacher who tore up the poems you wrote in class, who wrote harsh words on your report card so you'd get into unnecessary fights with your parents, and who all your class hates but have seen within the goodness of their hearts to forgive – Tom Truscott, what will YOU do to this man who has made racist jokes about your best friend Bob, confiscated your guitar for a fortnight and given you a combined total of 58 cuts of the cane, and one time gave you six in such a cruel way that you will remember it forever. What will you do to him?'

Mr Devlin, with the greaseback hair, steps forward.

'O God,' I reply, 'if it pleases you…', I say rolling up my sleeves, 'I would like to cane him as hard as I possibly can. I'd like to thrash my old teacher before the multitudes of people and the hosts of Heaven – for Lord, as you well know, he caned me publicly many times in front of the class, drawing blood once and still not stopping, making me cry when I was 13 when all I did was talk in class'.

God smiles. He's been waiting awhile for a little punk like me to stop all this bloody forgiving.

'Bend over!' I command Devlin.

And he bends before the class, the nation, the population of Planet Earth and the hosts of Heaven, poking his bum up that I may strike.

I pause and say, 'O Lord, one last request? May I unsheath the cane from behind the top of the blackboard in the same way as he always did? For I always found that anticipation so frightening when I was little.'

A fully furnished blackboard is instantly created by His own hand.

I unsheath that cane, the bamboo cane, from the top of the board. I then flail the air, swish-swish, as he waits - as we had to – then I rush towards Devlin and cut him with all my might.

It feels good. He jumps forward on the follow-thru, which gives me an excuse to whip him across the back of the knees for 'moving'. The 'extra' one, like he used to sneak on us.

'How many am I getting?' Devlin simpers.

'How many O Lord, may I give before exceeding the State Legal Limit?'

'Six.'

'Then Mr Devlin, I'm giving you the lot. Bend over.'

I take three steps back and slash the second cut. I hit him with all my strength. I want him to feel my rage. I'd love to give all 58.

I've never been happier.

'I wish you weren't doing this in front of the whole class…' he whimpers, '…not in front of the girls too'.

'In front of the girls, your wife, your kids, your parents, my friends, the angels, the history of the world and God,' I reply. 'After a while, we even got used to that awful pain on cold winter mornings. Like we got used to the terror of public thrashings. Bend over.'

After the third cut, I poke him in the chest with the tip of the cane and mimic him, 'I'm only doing it for your own good. Why aren't you showing me more respect? You've got a terrible attitude…!' Ha har.

No. 4 is a beauty. A masterclass stroke. I inflict the kind of pain that makes me wish I had a staffroom I could go back and boast to.

'Bend over again!' Slash. Another fine shot. I have to smile. His bottom lip begins to quiver while I spin around and take a bow to the whole Earth whose applause indicates this is great theatre.

The sixth swipe is also first class. It's as good a piece of caning as – say - Clapton's guitar work in *Crossroads.* It's as good as the organ in *Whiter Shade of Pale.* I leave him collapsed in the dirt, sobbing, kicking his legs, hurt, ashamed and magnificently caned.

'Thank you! Thank you!' I shout out to the hosts of Heaven, as I accept their huge round of applause. Pablo Picasso shakes my hand. Bob Dylan asks for my autograph. God thanks me very much. My class wants an encore, 'More! More! More!' And then I wake up.

I have a dream that I just caned my teacher.

For a while I even believed in Karma.

'Oh, by the way,' says God, when I'm out of my dream, 'Beatles manager, Brian Epstein has died. I want you to know that I had nothing to do with it'.

WHY DONTCHA GROW YER HAIR!
SHARP.

23

Land of 1000 Dancers

I have a dream.

I have a dream that all the brilliant minds, those we will never catch, have run off the road. We're all that's left. And we're famous.

I dream of a planet overpopulated with small unimportant things and awful musicians who breed. And it's closer than I think: small minds, technicians and insects.

Genius is in that grave over there. The epitaph reads, *Tread carefully, you're stepping on my balls.*

I dare not list the dead, the celebrity casualties. Jayne Mansfield has died in a terrible car crash. Dylan has had a motorpsycho nightmare.

I have a dream, a fear, that I'm rich and famous and occupying space that belonged to a once-clever ghost. Weirdly, I'm top of the pops.

I have become isolated, that no one may see me. I have a huge staff of record engineers, filmmakers, ghostwriters, image-creators, touch-up photographers and stand-in vocalists. I have mega hits. I am the most beautiful one. Bigger – as they say – than Elvis.

My body weight has doubled.

Thick rolls of stomach fat tremble and tumble over my trouser belt. I eat greasy food. I sweat oil. My tired eyes have seen every boring decadent thing.

Three naked nymphets lick the tiny veins at the back of my knees. But naked nymphets are not my hobby.

The pulsing rhythm of Rock music pounds from every speaker in my mansion. Gold records line my walls. Every desk is a piano. Every plate, a record. But music is not my hobby.

My hobby is vomiting. I do it all the time.

God is my employee, a short Indian handyman with a silly accent who says wise stuff when he carries out the garbage. How the world has turned. We've graduated demoted him and cut back his pay.

Can you believe, we used to listen to him all the time, in the yellow days when the sun still shone. He even used to sit on the throne on which I now sit. All the rich and famous people used to gather around his feet and sing, *All You Need is Love.* I was present too, standing way way up the back.

And then someone dies and there's a little gap.

Someone spots me - the drummer from Herman's Hermits I think – and gives me a break.

'Come here,' he says, 'Stand here, on the far edge of the group. Now that John Coltrane is dead, we need someone to fill his space.'

I put down my bucket and brush and, having nothing better to do, say yeah okay sure.

Then God (who is wise but not clever) asks us to sing *Blowin in the Wind.* We sing and sing it until the words became a chant and we forget its meaning. My shoes grow spikes and I step on the toes of the most talented people in the mob and I draw blood.

'I'm being called...' says a beautiful blond man (in the near-future). 'I'm taking my white teardrop guitar and planning to drown at the bottom of Eternity's great swimming pool of talent. My band hates me and I have lost the will to swim.'

'Hey man,' says a Rolling Stone, 'YOU! (meaning me...!) take another step up, cos we've all moved slightly forwards'.

That's how I spend those days, inching to the front.

Strange, with every loss, the Hall of Fame doesn't shrink, nor does its influence slide. It's God who is diminished.

In fact, with the passing of quality, the rich only get richer. People throw over their jobs as cost clerks and become players of new musical instruments where they only have to press an occasional button.

Sales reps become drummers by simply switching on machines. Beautiful idiots become sex symbols. Curtain designers become Great Artists. The best people are gradually extinguished. Everyone with talent is force-fed heroin and too dazed to speak. And in this brave new world, there is more money than anyone ever dreams of, new generations to feed.

Into this shuffle for position, I arrive.

Behind me, a host of people who understand the buttons – marketers, strategists, the prefects of Art and Music. Everyone has shorter hair. Everyone is older. The talent is almost drained.

Yet the kids still buy it in droves. I feel sick. I - who have traveled from the far edge into the ringside of the connoisseurs and opinion-makers - suddenly feel so sick.

I throw up. I heave. I chuck. I vomit. The art connoisseurs say it's a statement, so original, so 'says it all'.

They say, I am where Dada was heading - the meaning of life, as Sumo Sex-Machine Greasy performance art.

'It's the Shock of the New!'

It's *Avant-Garde*!'

Boastfully, I accept the accolades as creator of Vomit Art and Techno-Vomit Music. I am the greatest.

I have a dream that I am the most famous Rock Star in the history of the world. I spend my days eating deep fried anything, circled by a dozen uniformed women with guns.

Somewhere on the horizon, on the very edge of talent, are some young punks, spiky-haired warriors, the youth of the future who are making an Art of Noise. There's talk of old values, stagecraft, power chords and excitement.

I must destroy that challenge before it starts.

I command the technician on my right to invent a new rhythmic Blurt-o-Graph to divert the buying audience from listening to music.

GET THAT POOFTER
POW

24

My Back Pages

Banned from going anywhere good. Banned from Beethovens. Banned from Clayton's party. Grounded in Turramurra. Banned from the band.

It takes a while, but after a bit you get used to entertaining yourself in your bedroom with intimate things like your guitar, the book in which to scribble ideas and notes about *King Lear.*

Just as I'm getting used to being quarantined, I have to return to skool.

The first teacher I see is Bidwell who hopes I have been studying *Pride and Prejudice* by Jane Yuk Austen.

Think I'll pop in and say hi to Kennedy.

'Nice to have you back Tom,' he says.

Calder digs me out of the Art Room almost immediately and has a 'private chat' to me before I go see the Boss (who I must see to officially terminate my suspension, before going back to class). Calder says I've got to change my attitude, otherwise I'm fucked.

Well, he doesn't exactly say *fucked,* but that's what he's getting at. He reckons the assignment I did on the Peloponnesian War during my suspension is 'university standard', but I admit to him it's the only homework I did. Nothing for the other subjects, cept I read the middle bit of *King Lear. Nuncle* - I liked that.

Devlin opens the door, says something to Calder. Looks surprised to see me, eyes go straight to my hair. But he doesn't say anything cos I'm Calder's not his, for the moment.

Cut my throat later, I guess. Cut my thoughts.

Wandering around the verandah, Bob's pretty pleased to see me back, 'Hey man!'

'H'war ya?' I say.

'Got a coupla new records...'

'Oh yeah?'

'Son House an Lightin Hopkins.'

'Wow! Who again...?'

'An Sonny Terry too. D'ya hear what they did to Mark?'

'Yeah I did – sticking him in the Assembly Hall til he gets a haircut. But he won't cut his hair, no matter what. Really pisses off the Boss.'

'What else has bin goin on?'

'Had a practice without you - Samantha took over.'

'*Samantha?*'

'Yeah. She got Mark to sing a couple of songs and she sang a few of yours. But before you crack the absolute shits man, she's been pretty good at getting gigs'.

'Like?'

'St Ives Masonic Hall – opening for Phil Jones & the Unknown Blues!'

'Mark's taking over the vocals, is he?'

'Well, I don't think it's his idea.'

'It doesn't matter whose idea it is…if he's going along with it.'

'Look,' says Bob, 'I only joined this bunch of lunatics because of you'.

'Naah, I quit.'

'See the year out.'

'That's what the teacher's are telling me about skool!'

'Tom, if she takes over on vocals I'll quit too.'

'Maybe we could do something – jus you and me…?'

'This is what I reckon…' says Bob, '…doan quit yet though. The band is the only stable thing in your life. Do nothing - I reckon - until the year's out. Maybe we can do something together afterwards…?'

The word 'afterwards' brings me to wondering about HIS future, 'How's Louise?'

'Her ole man thinks we've broken up, but we've been seeing each other every second day over the last fortnight'.

'How'd I get to meet her?'

'You'll meet her, ah promise. It's tricky right now because she's not supposed to be anywhere I go.'

'Bloody parents!' I shake my head. 'What about the band?'

'Jus see how things pan out, okay…' and before Bob can finish his sentence he spots someone running towards us, straight from the Boss who's bin watchin us from the office verandah.

Bob and I see him coming and stroll off, to make it more difficult for the Boss's runner.

'Hey, you Tom!'

Can't hear.

The exhausted 2nd Former has to get to the Woodwork Building before he catches us, and he blurts, 'The Boss wants to see you Tom immediately!'

Big fucken deal.

'You…' the 2nd former says to Bob, 'the Boss wants you to *scoot.*'

‘Fine,’ Bob shrugs, gratified I guess, not to be called up for his hair. He can only get away with it if they classify it Aboriginal, ethnic or something. They’d want it shaved if they thought it was a Hendrix.

*

Cornered and summoned, I appear before the Boss - two weeks straight without a skool haircut. He checks socks, rings, sidelevers, shoes, all okay. But the hair?

‘Barely regulation length’ he says, cos he doesn’t want to send me straight back home.

The Boss says he wants me to make a goddamn apology speech to the staff before I am allowed to attend classes. A simple reassurance that I’ve turned over a new leaf and am prepared to show some skool spirit.

As he drones on, my mind wanders.

Strange that Adrian Jackson, Skool Captain, Sports Captain, Dux and winner of the Skool Citizenship Award once told he that he *hates* the Boss.

I couldn’t understand why a suck like him might hate the Boss until Adrian explained that he’s got more reason that me an Mark to hate him because he believed in the system more than we did.

Adrian says he’d love to be bad but he’s stuck being good. He’d rather be like us. I’d never thought of that before. I always figured the goodies were good because they were humans without a pulse.

Now, it seems even the angels are exploding.

‘The staff is prepared to…Thomas, are you listening?’

‘Yeah.’

‘Yes SIR!’

‘Yes, um sir.’

‘The staff is prepared to start you off on a clean sheet. All they want is some indication from you that you are prepared to play a positive role in school life. We’re right behind you young man. What more could you wish for?’

And Janet. Why does *she* obey the rules? What’s in it for her? She doesn’t do all this just for the badge.

No one’s that dumb. It’s some other reason? She hates that tough stuff. She hardly gives anyone lines. What the hell’s she playing along with it for?

I don’t understand John either. I can’t understand him being so straight at the start of the year and then throwing it away to support me against Hopkins. John says he’d like to get drunk with me, Mark and Bob.

What the hell does he wanna do that for?

'Are you listening to me!' The Boss bangs his fist on his desk and knocks over a plastic Jesus.

'Yes I am,' I reply.

'There's been a clampdown on students with bad attitudes. Nowadays your friend Mark spends his days in the Assembly Hall…'.

'Yeah, I know…'

'…defiance is one of the worst traits and Mark is defiant. You, Thomas, are not, you've got other problems, which is why we're prepared to give you another go. The staff is still right behind you boy, Mr Kennedy says you write poems…'

'…songs.'

'Well, words. So I'd like you to submit something to the School Magazine Committee. What do you say son? The honour of being published in your 1967 School Annual.'

'They're not that sort of lyrics,' I reply.

'We'll let Mr Bidwell be the judge of that, he's the expert. Submit your poems and he'll evaluate them. But…', he cocks a suspicious eyebrow as he stares at

– well, if I were a girl I'd reckon he's staring at my left tit. 'What's that in your shirt pocket? Not *cigarettes* I hope?'

'Just a cufflink box.'

'A what?'

'A cufflink box.'

'Now why would you be carrying such an item on your person?'

'It's where I keep my plectrums.'

'Your what? Show me.' I pull it out and hand it over.

He opens it suspiciously. 'Strange little plastic things…' says the Boss. 'What on earth are these used for? Nothing to do with drugs I hope?'

'No, they're plectrums for playing guitar.'

'Hmm…', he picks one out quite gingerly, then turns on his desk lamp and studies the Fender plectrum very very carefully. He smells it, touches it with his tongue, wraps it in a handkerchief and says, 'I think I might take it down to the Police Station to have it checked'.

'But…!'

'Right-o Thomas,' says the Boss, rubbing his hands together all businesslike. 'Just one last duty and you can go back to class. Accompany me to the staffroom where you can make a formal apology to the staff. We can catch them all right now before first period. Otherwise, you'll have to sit outside my office all day and I'll ask again tomorrow. What do you say son?'

I nod. I guess it means yes.

How would Keith Richards have handled this? Told the Boss to fuck off, I bet. That's why he's a Rolling Stone and I'm only Turramurra.

I wish I had more guts. Thousands and thousands of kids in America, no older than me, are saying NO to Vietnam and NO to racism. The Hippies even tried to levitate the White House. They can do anything they want. But me, I've nodded yes and am already tailing the Boss to the staffroom.

Juniors are pointing as me as we walk past. They think I'm a hero cos I got suspended, cos I'm in a band, cos of my hair and cos of the music. They have no fucken idea, do they?

'Good luck', says Janet as I walk past her.

'That's another thing…' says Bald Head, 'You've got to stop talking to girls'.

Bob crosses his fingers for me as I walk past him. The Boss sees it.

'That's another thing too…surround yourself with better companions - people who want to get ahead and make a buck'.

The guy who screwed the Alsatian walks past.

'Nice lad that...', says the Boss, '...my kind of guy. Try to spend more time with people like that'.

Into the staffroom now.

Seeing the Mighty Boss, the teachers stop their chitchat, close their books, stub out their cigs and gradually get around to paying attention to ME. I'm centre stage. I'm what happens next.

Christ I hate em. Bidwell the 'poetry expert' who's never heard of Ginsberg. Who won't have it that a third of Shakespeare's lousy sonnets were written to some boy, while the others were written to a Dark Lady, an Aboriginal woman from Alice Springs, I bet.

Then there's the Modern History teacher who reckons modern times ended with Metternich, Bismark and Kaiser Wilhelm and won't discuss Vietnam.

There's Irwin, the Junior Maths Master, a deadset drip.

Calder, giving me deep and meaningfuls. He looks bloody serious.

Hopkins, who won't look me in the eye.

Devlin, picking his nose.

And Kennedy, half-looking at me and half at whatever he's sketching.

The Boss calls them to order by tapping his Parker pen on a desk. He says stuff about me having learned the error of my ways, and that I've turned over a new leaf and wish to apologise to the staff for all the trouble I've caused.

The time has come for me to open my mouth and say something. Deep breath.

'Headmaster and all the teachers of this skool, especially Mr Hopkins, I'm sorry for all the trouble I caused...' cos that's as far as I can get without thinking about what to say next.

It's that word 'trouble'. *Say something about that.* 'I really don't like causing trouble, despite what you might all think'. Hmm, just a closing sentence required now, 'I promise to settle down and do my best for the rest of the skool year'. I've dunnit. I've betrayed myself again and I'm free. It's over.

But then another voice inside me wants to have its say. And just as the Boss is about to wrap it up, I find myself speaking some more. 'To be absolutely honest...'

'Oh no!' I can see on Kennedy's face. 'Sit down Tom! Now!' I see it on Calder's face too. But I've loosened my tongue and it won't go back in.

'...to be absolutely honest, I sometimes have very negative feelings about skool. Rules about hair length and uniform really bug me, cos I'm 18 years old. Every time I try to express these feelings to any the teachers, I can't - because I'm always scared of punishment, scared you'll tell my parents and scared of being expelled, which I don't want to happen because I really want to see the skool year out. So, when you tagged me with a *bad attitude* you were probably right. I really believe that we should be allowed to sit next to girls on the trains.

I really believe growing our hair should be permitted – we don't tell you how to wear yours…!'

The Boss looks like he's had quite enough. Best wrap it up.

'Headmaster and teachers, I'm glad I told the truth because you might now believe me when I say I'm sorry for causing all this trouble. I didn't mean to upset Mr Hopkins or anyone else. I'll try my hardest to stay out of trouble from now on and…'.

'Thank you Thomas!' says the Boss, looking at his watch.

I'm back!

WE ARE THEM... THEY ARE US...

MORATORIUM!

25

The Letter

Ancient History class and Calder is explaining Greek democracy, which sounds nothing like what we think democracy means. Eventually I get to Anarchy, not that it's Greek, but it's something Calder touched on earlier in the year and never really discussed.

'Do you still reckon you and your generation can do anything you want?' he asks the class, but he's really targeting me.

'Yep,' I reply. 'Even Mr Devlin reckons there's gonna be future shock. The times they are a-changin fer sure.'

'Only those at the top of the pile can do whatever they want and get away with it,' he replies, 'Read your Bury text and you'll see that even they can't always get away with it, look what it did for Socrates!'

'He did all right. We're reading his stuff two thousand - or whatever - years later!'

'So what's the answer Tom?'

'Ah, turn on, tune in, drop out,' is my answer.

'And having done that, how to you stay alive?'

'You can't, if money is concerned. But if there wuz no more money, no rules, no government, there'd be no more war. Our governments kill us.'

'If you actually toppled the government, do you know what happens next?'

'What?'

'It creates a power vacuum, which someone invariably fills. Most power vacuums get filled by tyrants. In this country we're fortunate to have a democracy. Here, we're free, compared to many others. As free as anyone has ever been. You complain about rules. Yet you've got no Berlin Wall, no Josef Stalin, no Secret Police and - no sudden invasion from Sparta!' he says, returning the rave to Sparta V & Athens 431-404BC.

*

Next class is Devlin's vocational guidance shit. I sit with Janet. Devlin is telling us something about bloody missionaries in the New Hebrides and that we should give into the voice of god if we can feel it within.

I can't. So I whisper to Janet instead. 'We've got to turn the skool marches into a protest march'.

'I'm worried about you,' she says. 'You've only got seven more weeks and you're shooting off your mouth again'.

'Make love not war - is that shooting my mouth off?

'It is to teachers.'

I whisper, 'I've got a cousin in Vietnam, He'll be home soon. Me & Mark could get picked in the ballot to take his place. It's just not right. My cousin's a fighter, we're known cowards'.

'The main thing for you right now is to get good grades in the HSC.'

'Good grades don't matter if you're dead or if you can't live with yourself because you've killed someone'.

'Don't rag me Tom, you're not serious enough as a person to be worrying about stuff like that.'

'What are you two whispering about?' asks Devlin.

'Vocational guidance sir,' I pipe up, 'Weighing up the Army as a career option.'

'Hmm,' he growls.

Then I tell Janet all about Beethoven's Disco on Sundays and Jeff St John & the Yama. I brag about being friends with someone who went to court for breaking and entry. Tell her I've been drunk several more times since the party. And that I'm not a virgin any more.

'Will you two stop talking!' he snaps.

So we write notes.

After a bit, he does a doubletake, fixes on Janet and asks, 'Is that a note Tom passed you?'

'Yes sir.'

'Then give it here thank you.'

Hand outstretched he waits for Prefect Janet to walk to the front of the class and hand it across, but she doesn't.

'Did you hear what I said? The note!'

Janet doan move. She just stares at the floor.

'I DEMAND you give me that note! Get up here!' God, this greaseback can yell.

She walks down the front of the class and just stands there, head bowed in silence, like some Catholic saint.

'Now – hand me the note!'

She slips it inside her bra, where he can't take it out.

'What's the big deal?' John whispers.

I reply, 'It says *I fucked Shane.'*

'O god…' John shakes his head, '…you're gone!'

Fuck – that word teachers and parents have told us must never be written or said. Root, screw, 'have intercourse with', poke, shag and a whole list of words that mean exactly the same are 'naughty' words. Fuck is filth.

Bloody – is not good. It's worth about 100 lines.

Shit – means you get about two cuts.
But *fuck* means expulsion because the person saying it has got a potty-mouth and a filthy mind.

It's actually more okay to fuck than to say fuck. Sooner or later everyone fucks. My teachers fuck. Colin's parents fuck. Janet's parents fuck. Even Jenny's parents fuck. Everyone's parents fuck. But none of them are dirty-filthy-minded enough to say the word. Say it around skool and you're finished. And if Janet hands that note over, that's exactly what I am. Nothing would make Devlin happier than to capture a note with that word written. That's the only reason teacher's read the little notes that get passed around in class. They're hoping for *fuck* in your handwriting. Then they've gotcha.

Devlin raises his voice, 'Gimme that note!' His hands are shaking a bit, cos he's finding it difficult to cope with Saint Janet, head bowed.

My head is bowed too, ashamed. Not ashamed of what I've written. Ashamed I've got someone into trouble they don't deserve. Ashamed that I've put her in a position where she's got to choose between obeying the rules or protecting me. If I had any guts I'd walk down the front, ask for the note back, eat it and run with the consequences.

'Are you defying me Janet?'

Still no answer.

'Go to the headmaster's office and wait there!' She's driven him crazy. She's picked the loophole in the system - that you can always appeal to a higher court.

She won't defy the system, I know she won't. She'll hand the note over to the Boss, but not to Devlin. *Not to Devlin* is pretty important because at least Devlin feels cheated, which is the main thing.

Janet leaves the room and heads for the main office. Devlin tells us to read from our textbooks while he tails her.

'What happened then?' everyone wants to know.

*

'Sorry Tom, I had to do it,' she says when she comes back.

'What's the outcome?'

'Devlin wants me suspended. He insists I lose my prefect's badge, but being a prefect doesn't mean anything to me any more. After I finish skool, I won't even remember it.'

'I'm the opposite,' I reply, 'I don't think I'll ever forget skool. Being caned. Writing 300 lines in one night. Standing outside the Boss's office for ages. I don't think anything that happens to me for the rest of my life will ever be as bad as going to school.'

'Unless you get sent to Vietnam…' Mark chips in.

'Unless I get sent to Vietnam,' I reiterate.

'Well,' says Adrian, 'some of us are going to be conscripted. Some of us are going to get married and divorced. Some will have sick kids. Some might even die young or somethin. School's a small drama Tom, I bet that's all it is.'

'What's that gotta do with Janet losing her badge?' asks Sue.

'It's because she didn't hand over the note I wrote.'

'Why not?'

'Because I wrote fuck in it.'

'Then it's all your fault Tom,' says Adrian.

'I guess so…'.

'You're a walking H-Bomb Tom, you really are.'

'Always getting others into trouble…'.

'Not *always.'*

'Well,' says John, 'We don't have to take it!'

'Too right!' says Mark, now back in class cos he snipped a bit off his hair.

'Jus put up with it,' I tell them, 'I'm as good as gone now'.

'It's not about you Tom,' says Adrian, 'Janet's the one we're worried about. They're gonna punish her for something you did, you frigging basket!'

'Leave Tom alone,' says Janet.

Suddenly the whole class starts muttering about going on strike if Janet is punished, but I don't really join in. My opinion doesn't count any more. I'm expelled and I know it.

'We'll all go on strike for Janet,' says the Skool Captain.

There's a bald shadow in the doorway.

A sudden hush.

In walks the Boss. His eyes immediately locate me in the room, then flick around the classroom.

'Is there a problem Adrian?'

'Yes sir, there definitely is.'

'What is it?'

'Well sir,' says the School Captain, 'None of it's Janet's fault. That's true and honest. We all saw what happened and the others'll back me up. We don't think Janet deserves punishment.'

'True sir,' Janice chips in, 'Mr Devlin pushed it too far...'

'Don't talk to me like that about another teacher!' he snaps. 'Janet WILL lose her badge, but only for a week.'

'What do you mean suh?'

'I mean, she'll lose it as a token of our disapproval for her defying a teacher. Then she'll get it back. Things have to be done in a certain way because that's how society works. Otherwise there'd be anarchy. Adrian, do you believe in anarchy?'

'No sir, of course not sir.'

'You Greg?'

'No suh.'

'Sue?'

'No.'

'How bout you Jenny? Do you believe people should rush into the streets and break things just because they don't like the rules?'

'Of course not.'

'Janice, would you like to see this school's reputation harmed in any way?'

'No.'

'Now what's all this talk of a strike?'

They all hang their heads, ashamed.

'Then that only leaves one person for me to deal with,' says the Boss, 'Thomas Truscott…!'

'Yeah.'

'Remember this?' From his inside coat pocket he produces my note.

I SEE THE POPE WANTS PEACE IN VIETNAM
...MUST BE TURNING COMMO.
FIEND RAPES JUMBO
PICTURE
NEWS REVIEW
SHARP.

26

There Won't Be Many Coming Home

Expelled.

That lousy feeling that you've let everyone down. *What will the neighbours say?* That shame upon the family. The hassle for my ole man. I won't get to sit my Level 1 Ancient History exam for Calder. Plus I'm a fucken disgrace for writing the banned word that every mother hopes her son will never stoop to using. The tears.

The Boss phoned my ole man straight away, so the family already knows the skool's side of the story before I'll get home. Nothing for it now, cept to get off skool premises.

That inevitable question will come up, 'Who's Shane?' Mum'll ask it.

'A junkie hooker thief' mightn't go down too well. So I'm not sure what my hopeless answer's gonna be. 'A nice PLC girl' isn't gonna work cos they're sure to remember the name from Stu's breaking & entry. Should this come up and I'll be the kid who'll stoop at nuthin.

Is my boy a drug addict?
Has he got VD?
I'll be in-and-out of every clinic in town!

I can't bear to think about my reception when I get home, so I go to the Art Room and see Mr Kennedy one last time. He's very disappointed to see me go. All alone in his office cluttered with paperback books, half finished pictures, framing material, art jackets and a section for big Art books with titles like, *The Language of Graphics* and *Australian Painting.* On the far wall is a repro of Vincent's *On the Road to Tarascon.* Kennedy reckons the original was blown to bits in World War 2.

'And yet we still fight each other!'

'I thought your generation was keen on war Mr Kennedy?'

'Call me Morriss – you're not a schoolboy any more.' Wow, just like that and *I'm not a schoolboy any more*! Nothing about me has changed. All it took was the E-word from the Boss. Hmm...If I can call him Morris, maybe I can smoke on skool premises?

'I said, I thought your generation was keen on war?'

'Why on earth should you think that?'

'Those war films, the news, the Anzac thing and, of course Vietnam.'

'There was a lot of camaraderie that made...ah...war a life defining experience. Your parents are probably still living under the cloud of a war that is only 23 years old. It must have been...er...the worst time in their lives...' says Mr Kennedy, '...your generation didn't invent peace, justice and freedom too, I'm sure that's the Anzac message too'.

'But you're different…!'

'Different to whom?'

'Different to other teachers and parents. You're like a Beatnik who became a teacher.'

'Well, I was never a Beatnik…although I did attend East Sydney Tech…' he pauses, 'No one likes Vietnam, not your parents, not the other teachers. But it's all about fear. Fear that the…ah…Commies will keep moving south. It's a small war meant to stop a bigger war.'

'So you're for it then?'

'Of course I'm not. It's good for the US economy, nobody's blind to that…'.

'My cousin Ken's in Vietnam. He's coming home in a couple of days. He's the brave one in the family.'

'I'm not for Vietnam at all. I'm on the side that judges people as kindly as possible. I'm on…ah…your side, I'm on your…ah…cousin's side too. All your cousin's doing is something for his country. He's not enjoying the killings. Neither are…er…the Americans!'

Then I say something stupid about make luv not war. Something about Cousin Ken being a conformist, and Morriss says I'm still a kid to blabber on like that.

'Do you know why you've been expelled?' he asks. 'You've been expelled because you're…er…immature in areas where your classmates are more mature, and mature in areas where your classmates are less mature. Sometimes…ah…see where you're coming from, like when you stood up against Devlin. I know why you did that, I just watched it play itself out like a waltz…'.

'…actually, that was Janet who stood up to him, not me'.

'Maybe I was once a bit like you, I wasn't a Beatnik any more than you are…ah…what did you say you were – a Mod? Hippie? Maybe I tried hard and didn't make it as an artist. Maybe that's why I'm a teacher. But one day you'll have your band and one day I will have my art show. Let me read you something…'

He picks up the book on his desk, it's the book of Vincent's letters to Theo. He reads:

Now for more than five years – I do not know exactly how long I have been more or less without employment wandering here and there. You say, 'Since a certain time you have gone down, you have deteriorated, you have not done anything'. Is this quite true? It is true that occasionally I have earned my crust of bread, occasionally a friend has given it to me in charity. I have lived as I could, as luck would have it, haphazardly. It is true that I have lost the confidence of many; it is true that my financial affairs are in a sad state; it is true that the future is only too gloomy; it is true that I might have done better; it is true that I've lost time in terms of earning my bread; it is true that even my studies are in rather a sad and hopeless condition, and that my needs are greater – infinitely greater than my possessions. But is this what you call 'going down', is this what you call 'doing nothing'?

For the moment it seems that things are going very badly with me, and it has already been so for a considerable time and may continue awhile in the future; but after everything has seemed to go wrong, perhaps a time will come when things will go right. I don't count on it, perhaps it will never happen; but if there is a change for the better, I should consider it so much gain. I should be contented. I should say 'At last! You see there was something after all!'

I think that everything which is really good and beautiful – of inner moral, spiritual and sublime beauty in men and their works – comes from God, and all that which is bad and wrong in men and in their works is not of God, and God does not approve of it.

But I always think that the best way to know God is to love many things. Love a friend, a wife, something – whatever you like you will be on your way to knowing more about him; that is what I say to myself. But one must love with a lofty and serious intimate sympathy, with strength, with intelligence; and one must try always to know deeper, better and more. That leads to God, that leads to unwavering faith.

If I have come down in the world, you, on the contrary, have risen. If I have lost the sympathy of some, you on the contrary, have gained it. That makes me very happy – I say it in all sincerity –and always will. If you hadn't seriousness or depth, I would fear that it would not last; but as I think you are very serious and of great depth, I believe that it will. But I should be glad if it were possible for you to see me as something more than an idle man of the worst type.

For the present, I shake hands with you, thanking you for the help you have given me. Ever yours

Vincent

Kennedy's head is bowed like he's just recited a prayer.

I look at his rough hands, the clay and paint under his fingernails. His head down, greying hair, I want to join him in that prayer. I wanna pray he has his exhibition. Pray that he gets out of teaching skool. Pray that he meant *me* when he said, 'I shake hands with you, thanking you for the help you have given me'. I hope I was of some help to him. Just as I hope that I was a fucken nuisance to all the others in this godawful place that's chucked me out.

'That was a letter from Vincent to Theo,' says Mr Kennedy, slowly regaining his composure.' And I can't say goodbye to you with a finer message'. He extends his hand. Shake.

'Ciya Morriss.'

'Goodbye Tom, I've enjoyed having you in my classes. You're a great kid.'

We both know it's over. I'll never see Mr Kennedy again. He goes with the skool.

Expelled.

Mum says she doesn't know what she's done wrong in life to cop a son like me.

Expelled.

Well, it's not quite that cut-and-dry. True, I can't go back to that skool, but my father phones the NSW Education Department and finds that I've attended sufficient classes to sit the HSC if he can get the Boss to sign something. True, I won't be sitting the exams at my ole skool, but I might be able to transfer to a NSW State skool or tech college. I CAN sit my HSC exams – somewhere else - and if I do okay, I can still make uni.

As a second alternative, Dad has another crack at offering me a job as a property manager, for starters. No selling - just managing the rental properties. Not difficult. But I would have to keep my hair short. I refuse. As payback, Dad says in the lead-up to the HSC, I have to spend every day studying and he's got an office for me out the back, where I can study 9-5. That's like my 'family punishment' for being expelled - going to the office with Dad. Still, I don't have to wear skool uniform and he doesn't police my hair with the same enthusiasm as the Boss.

Great timing. The Family Hero is coming home from Vietnam precisely when I get expelled. Cousin Ken, who left home at 16, fought a war by the time he was my age, cut his own grass in life, is coming to our place for a family get-together.

'What did you get expelled for,' Auntie is sure to say.

'For writing the word *fuck* Auntie,' I won't say.

It's the day of Ken's coming home party. He looks thinner, meaner and stronger, with an edginess he didn't used to have. Like he's punchy or somethin. Everyone wants to talk to him, even me.

His Mum says I look woeful. Auntie Edna grabs my hair and tugs it, 'Are you trying to be one of those Yippies?' It's a bit of an ordeal but I feel I get off fairly light because thank god she didn't ask about my expulsion. She skirts the subject by asking what I plan on doing next? I tell her I wanna go to uni. She pulls a face. *Going to uni* might sound great in some circles but not in our family, where the thing to be is 'self-made'. For them, 'going to uni' is like saying I plan on being a ratbag protester, a poofta and probably a bloody Commie.

Ken's fiancée is sure pleased to have him back. She's about the happiest person in the room and friendly to me. Her name is Alice and she always checks me out about girlfriends. I tell her I haven't got one. I tell her that I like Janet in one sort of way and Salli in different way. Then my expulsion comes up which leads to the wording of my note.

'Did you really shag her?' she whispers.

'Yes, I did,' I confess. Hooray, I've found the one person in the family who thinks it's great that I did ut. I walk through the specifics with Alice – she unzipped my fly, she got on top of me and so on - then I pester Alice with. 'Did I do it right?'

'Tom, it doesn't really matter…'.

'Well, I kinda thought it might.'

So I grab a lemonade and move across the room to Ken's ole man, Uncle Jim, who is pretty easy to take. He slaps me on the shoulder – whack – and just about bowls me over cos he's big. He doesn't talk me down because I mucked up skool. He just asks about how much money the band makes in a night. I tell im the Redfern figure.

'There's always recording,' he says, 'the bands that make money get recording contracts, you need to find out how they do that?'

'Well, a guy called Neil mentioned that he knew the guy who owns Linda Lee, a record company…'.

I tell Uncle Jim I'm into writing lyrics, like a singer called Bob Dylan. He seems puzzled about that, so I name the Beatles. Everyone knows the Beatles. Songs like *When I'm 64* are about the words, I think. 'I'll stick it on the turntable, it's Music Hall music, you might like it uncle…'.

I arrive at the stereo precisely when Ken does. I've got the *Sgt Pepper* LP in my hand, he's got a Digby Richards single in his.

'Good being home n that, I s'pose…?'

'Yeah,' he replies.

'You're not going back are ya?'

'No, I go back to my unit at South Head.'

I'm not sure what to say next to a Returned Soldier. 'It must be strange being back, no one shooting at you n that...?' Is that what you say to a soldier. (I dunno.)

'It's a bit strange, I s'pose,' he says, picking up on the theme, 'I woke up the other night after hearing a train go by and thought, *That CAN'T be right, we just hit that railway yard a week ago.* Strange things like that...' he drifts off, then – as if he suddenly realizes it's me he's talking to – he turns all prickly. 'But what's your story? I hear you got yourself chucked outta school?'

'Yeah, but you know what teachers are like...'.

'I know what *you're* like!'

'Well, you're not exactly perfect, Bangkok n that...!' I've got to watch him. If I cheek him out too much, he might clip me.

'What about Bangkok?' He doesn't like that.

'Um nuthin.'

'It's a bit more exciting than growing long hair and passin smutty notes to girls!' That's sorted me, I guess. I don't think I'll bother with *Sgt Peppers.*

He sticks on his record and announces to the room, 'Here's a song called *Aussie Bush Hat...'* which is a spoken word kinda thing about sad war stuff, which I find boring and I tell Alice so.

'This is the daggiest song I've ever heard!' I whisper, while everyone else pays attention.

'Shut up Tom, it's about Ken's friend who got killed rescuing a kid.'

'Oh...!' I clap my hand over my mouth.

'Yeah,' says Ken, ignoring me, opening a beer and addressing the family. 'That song's about Ian Brown who got killed in Berea, a village just outside Nui-Dat. The Viet-Cong got a young kid, split her up the guts and threw her in the middle to get our doctors out there. Of course Browny went. It was a deadset trap and he knew it. They opened up on him. And by the time Browny got back to base to base camp there wasn't too much left in him.'

'You actually *saw* that!'

'Yes Tom,' he answers gravely, 'I did. And that's what the song is about, something pretty real to me'.

'Hmmm...' I go back to chatting to Alice about sex. I tell her all about Stu and Shane, Mark and Samantha, Bob and Louise. She wants to know why Bob's isn't allowed to see Louise. She's already guessed it's cos he's black and she doan like it.

'He's just as white as he is black,' she reasons.

'Same dog, different log!' I laugh.

She contradicts, 'No, that's not right. You only say that when siblings have the same *mother.* Bob and his siblings have the same *father...'*

'Look, it's cos he's black, but that's not the only reason...' I explain. 'His hair has gotta come into it somewhere. Some of my other friends aren't allowed to date their girlfriends either, and they're not black. Yair, it's their hair.'

Alice always wants to know who's doing it. Mark and Samantha certainly are. 'What about Bob and Louise?'

'Dunno...' (I really don't.) '...but I reckon they would be, pro'bly. Keep it quiet. Don't even tell Ken.'

'Hah! Like he'd care!

Ken's over in the corner with the Men. Blah blah blah, I can hear him loud and clear, '...I only did it cos I was in the Regular Army and it was part of my job - thrill seeking. But you hoped you were doing someone some good while you were over there...'. Blah blah blah. Army tawk.

Then my ole man has his turn - the Kokoda Trail - how the Aussie is a special kind of soldier and the Yanks respected the Aussie Bush Hat cos we had our own way of problem-solving. Rough n ready our boys were. ARE. Then Dad sees me walk past...not exactly 'rough n ready'. Never mind, he continues. Although the Aussies had to retreat, we captured it – whatever 'it' was – and a few of Dad's mates got killed too during the course of the war. He brags. Then Dad goes to the fridge and comes back with three beers – for uncle, Ken, himself but not me. 'Any of you girls want a drop of bubbly...?' He calls across the room, '...it's over there'. He points. The girls – that's Mum, auntie, Grandma and Alice (but not my little sister Jilly) – all huddle around the bottle on the sideboard and make jokes about having a little drinky and how 'naughty' that is, in the afternoon. The men stand no such ceremony, they just pull themselves another fucken beer and gulp it.

Now it's Uncle's turn to talk about his war. He's the only one who got hit. He talks about his old war wound, which no one's ever noticed. But yes, this afternoon and after three beers, he did to keep the Evil Hun from our doorstep. He did it for King & Country. Remember King George VI? And his brother, Edward? Now there's a story! 'But you young fellas wouldn't know what we're talking about...!' he laughs.

Then after half a glass of whatever the women are drinking, Auntie has a bit of a moment, throwing her arms around her boy and sayin again (she's already dunnit twice) how wonderful it is to have him safe in one piece, thank gawd, which is how she says god. Ken pats his Mum on the head, but after she goes on too long, he looks wildly around the room, for an escape hatch p'raps. When Mum joins the hug, Ken's really trapped. Then, thinking it's a group hug, Jilly joins in and hugs Ken's legs. He's physically holding them ALL up, relieved I'm sure that Grandma isn't getting out of her armchair to join in. Big cheer for Ken and the boys from Vietnam! Hoorah! These are the types that made Australia great! Yay! More beers! Then I overhear my father say, 'While your son's out there doing somethin for the country, mine got himself chucked outta skool. Look at the hair on im willya!'

'I do wish you men would stop drinking!' Mum pipes in, pouring another little one for Grandma.

'No,' my father rants, 'I'm bloody serious! The Commies are almost banging on our doors and…'.

'Enough!' says Mum. Then, abruptly changing the subject she says, 'It was very nice hearing your song Ken, and now that you've explained it, why don't you play it again so we can really appreciate its message'.

'Well I tell ya,' says Ken, 'That song sure means a lot to me. He was my mate Browny was'.

That fucken song again. Ker-yst! It reminds me of *The Ballad of the Green Beret* by Sgt Barry Sadler. *Sgt Peppers* is the only sergeant I respect.

'Good words,' says my ole man, about Ken's choice. 'It actually means something – Tom, are you takin notes?'

'Stuff off!' I reply, 'I wouldn't expect you to understand Bob Dylan!'

'No one understands Bob Dylan, he sings through his nose!'

'Stop this at once!' Mum exclaims.

'The whole trouble with this country,' Dad carries on, 'is that after Menzies, no one's got any balls. The skool's are a free-fer-rawl. Look at what's happened to Tom! I tell ya...' he says, winking at Ken, '...10 years ago it wasn't nearly as hard to get approvals for subdivisions as it is now. Mount Colah was going ahead until some desko slowed it down. The whole country's going to the pack!'

'Any good buys out that way?'

'You come an talk to me when your ready,' he puts his arm on Ken's shoulder. 'I'll look after you mate. Get your Low Interest Army Loan sorted and I'll do the rest...'

'Me and Alice were thinking...?'

And Dad goes to the fridge again. Uncle is singing *When the Boy from Alabama Meets the Girl from Gundagai,* 'Remember that one?' he asks. 'Joy Nichols it was. I bet I've still got that 78.' Then they all start talking about having a singalong and Auntie sez. 'Tom, get your guitar and play us a tune'.

'AND!' shouts Dad, nearly tripping over the couch, 'when you've finished in the Army, a guy like you could do a whole lot worse than getting a real estate license!'

'Got your guitar Tom?' reminds Auntie.

'I don't WANT him to get his guitar!' my ole man snaps. 'I've heard too much of that bloody guitar over the past months. *Tear down the cenotaph in Martin Place!* Yes, Tom wrote that! On his bloody guitar!'

'Well, not...!'

'*YOU* wrote that?' I reckon Ken was gunning for me the minute he arrived. Now he's got his excuse.

'Why don't you men take it easy and drink a nice cup of tea and have an Arnotts,' says Mum, standing between my father and the fridge. 'We've run out of beer'.

'Naah, we aven't...' says Dad.

'We've run out of beer!' she says with that air of finality he never contradicts.

'But we *can't* have run out of sherry?' says Grandma, waving her little glass.

Back to me again. Ken going *you wrote those words?* And me burbling something about peace.

'Listen son,' Dad turns to me, 'what you're proposin is unnatural. When you see your family and friends under threat then you *ought* to want to fight'.

'As far as I'm concerned,' says Ken, 'all those protest marches are backed by political people who pay university student yip-yips to cause trouble'.

'Get them hyped up on drugs!' adds Dad. 'Let's go knock this! Let's go knock that!'

'Half of them,' sez Ken, 'if you asked them why they're protesting, they wouldn't have a clue! All these uni kids carrying on. *Nuthin else on at night, let's go down to a protest rally, smoke a bit of pot, who knows – we may be able to bash a cop or roll a car, kick someone who's not lookin and git our jollies for the night. Because it's Saturday night and there's nuthin on television – so let's go an annoy every other bastard!*'

'Enough Ken!' That's Auntie.

'You know what the Army does to conscripts?' says Dad, mocking me, 'they flush their heads down the loo and cut their hair!'

'Not true,' Ken contradicts, 'if a uni student comes in who's gonna buck the system, he gets hauled into line quick-smart. I certainly had nuthin to do with haircutting or anythin like that. That's the hairdresser's job. But everyone who joins the Army gets their hair cut short. It's a standard thing, whether you're a uni student, a Regular or a Nasho. But I've always hated long hair... it's very handy if you get into a fight'.

‘Ken!’

‘....it gives you something to *hold!* And you Tom – you need a bloody good haircut!’

‘No!’ shrieks Alice.

I’m outta the room in a flash, down the corridor and into the bathroom, which I lock. Ken and Dad beat on the door. Bang bang. I can hear Dad shouting something about scissors. Ken bursts the lock and grabs me easily. The women are screaming at him as he drags me into my bedroom, chucks me on the bed, knocks over my guitar, sends my records sprawling and holds me down.

Dad’s got the scissors. Snip snip. I shake my head around, hoping he draws blood cos then he’ll really cop it from Mum. Snip snip. He’s cutting anything – sides, top, anything. And Cousin Ken holding me tight, even though Alice is hitting him on the back and yelling at him to stop.

Do they think this haircut will change anything?

No.

Cutting my hair won’t change a fucken thing.

We will never conform.

We will never get straight jobs.

We will never listen to Country & Western music.

We will never go to war.

We will never worship Capitalism.

We will never drink their beer.

We will never talk their smut.

We will never wear suits.

We will never stop wanting to get stoned.

We will never, ever give up.

Mum is *really* upset. Auntie is furious.

Still, my hair is ruined. They’ve made me look like a prefect.

They’ve also broken the neck of my guitar.

*

Much later, when Ken, Alice, Auntie & Uncle and Grandma have gone, Dad taps on my bedroom door and sits on the end of my bed. He picks up the pieces of my busted cheap Jap guitar and stares at the broken bits.

‘What’s the best guitar you can buy?’ he asks.

‘A Gibson Firebird,’ I answer.

‘Fair enough,’ he sighs, ‘I’m buying you one’.

27

The One in the Middle

Louise is preggers. Bob calls around and tells me. We walk to the park and talk about it, then back to my place to talk about it some more.

The parents and teachers are shocked and disgusted at what Bob & Louise've done. That's the end of Bob's skool year, as well as mine. They talk about Bob & Louise behind their backs, taking the trouble to count back the months to figure out whether they did it in August or September or whenever. Bob & Louise will *HAVE* to get married. That's how it's done in these parts. Instead of saying 'we're getting married' Bob & Louise will say they 'had to'. If they don't of course, the baby will be an illegitimate bastard no-account kid.

Bob & Louise are the big winners of 1967. From not being allowed to say hello to each other on buses, Louise's ole man is insisting Bob marries his daughter. There's a lesson right here to be learned about people & life. But buggered if I can understand it. Bob says they'll be married in January. The band is over now *fer sure*. I suggest that marriage needn't change a thing. Louise can stay home and mind the little tacker while Bob comes to band practice and gigs. But he reckons that's not fair on Louise, or something. Well, that's a newie.

The phone rings. It's Mark, phoning from Jay's place to say we've got a gig this Saturday night. He adds that we're a support for Phil Jones & the Unknown Blues and if we play, we might meet Phil as a bonus. Mark says, 'But we can't play it without you an Bob, Quit later if you really want to Tom, but we haven't got time to get a new line-up'. Yeah wow okay – but only if Samantha stays well away from the mike. Sure.

'Yer know somethin...' I tell Bob when Mark gets off the line, '...I really like those guys. I'm sorry skool's over - and with it the band. I don't know what I'll do about music next year...?'

'You don't *have* to play in a band to be a muso,' says Bob, 'Folk music is coming in inna big way. You could just do solo spots and play anything you bloody-well like on your own.'

'In a way, a band's an excuse to hang out with mates. A Boy's Club - isn't that what bands are about?

'Only if you want it to be, I don't see it that way. Louise plays flute and sings a bit, maybe we'll form a duo. You could do something like that instead.'

'Oh I don't know Bob...I don't know what I wanna be. I wanted to be Stevie Wright when I was 15 but now I think I'd rather be a Rock Poster Artist. Maybe go to Art School instead of uni, I dunno...?'

'Ha! Your Dad'd bloody luv that!'

'I used to wanna have a hit single. That was a bit of an idea around the time we wrote *Communist Girls,* but it went nowhere.'

'Well,' says Bob, responsible-like, 'I used to want a hit single too, whereas now I think raising a kid is pretty important'.

'If you'll do Saturday night, I'll do it too...'

'Okay.'

'Then I'll phone Mark back and tell im yes!'

'No probs with me mate, I never said I wouldn't play. All I said was when the kid's born, the kid comes first.'

'Maybe - if things settle down - maybe you and me can form the new Blitz. Get another drummer to free you up to play guitar. I'll find someone. And we'll check that manager-guy Neil talked about. The one who runs Linda Lee Records. We can try to cut a single.'

'Naa mate,' Bob replies, 'I'll do anything you like this year, but when 1968 comes round, count me out.'

'You know what?'

'Whut?'

'I wanna leave home immediately exams are done. I wanna piss off to Melbourne. Maybe Clayton wants to come. Or Mark. Or Jay. We can look Stu up.'

'Ah, Stu!' spits Bob.

'Jay'll be innit fer sure. Cos he doesn't give a stuff about his job. Mark too, once he's done with skool, he'll be ready for anythin.'

'And Clayton?'

'We'll he's kinda serious about his apprenticeship...'

So I phone Mark and Jay to tell them to count me in. (Bob can tell em he's pregnant later, in his own time.)

*

Next, we go over to Jay's place, practice eight songs, decide what to wear and head off to the St Ives Masonic Hall. Jay brings no one, I bring Salli, Mark brings Samantha. And Bob brings Louise. First time we meet her.

Louise is a blonde waif. Bare feet, floral dress, yellow flowers in her hair. She carries a rag doll around in her handbag. She's shy and Bob's proud. Salli likes her. They go off together and have a yak while we do sound checks. George – lead singer of The Mob – jokes around with Clayton and Jay, his old classmates from Normo High. The sound guy keeps asking me to go back to the mike and to stop wandering off until he's gotten it together. Doesn't seem to matter how hard I call 'eu-calyp-tus 1-2-3' into the mike, he always seems frustrated.

'Fer him, that's normal,' says George.

'Surprising how things pick up in front of an audience,' laughs Mark, getting his hair perfect.

'They give the ole nerves a bit ova lift,' I reply, fiddlin with a plastic nose someone left backstage.

'Are you ready then?'

'Ready as we'll ever be, I reckon!'

George yells out, 'Anyone fer a teabag?'

'Yeah, I'll av one,' says Mark.

'Got any proper drink?' asks Jay. Then he calls to Clayton. They go for a spin to the Pymble Pub. Ah, the quest for bourbon. Salli and Louise go along for the ride. But Samantha sticks around, giving lots of orders to the sound guy and running through our song list. 'Do *Heart Full of Soul* – Mark, you sing that really well. I could join you on the chorus...'.

'I think Tom can handle most of the singing tonight,' he snaps.

She goes all thingy on him. 'But the people want to hear *you* Mark...come on sweetie, don't chicken out on me tonight. And dedicate one to me, say *I'd like to dedicate this one to...'*

'Listen Sam,' says the mike guy, 'Get off the bloody stage!'

'*I beg your pardon!'* she snaps, whacking her hands on her hips and looking to Mark for support.

'Do like he says willya!' he snaps, 'We haven't got time for all this!'

'Oh thank you very much!' And off she goes. Doan know where. Then Clayton, Jay, Salli & Louise come laughin back with a proper bottle of bourbon, not a hip flask. Jay barely gets to tune his guitar when the audience starts arriving. After the first dozen are though the door, we reckon we're hot to trot, and go out the back where we hang out til 8.00 precisely. No one seems to give a fuck about Samantha, not even Mark.

'D'ya reckon we'll get the rhythm right in the bass break?'

'Yeah, I do.'

'There's that change of pace...?'

'A longer stop on the B p'raps?'

'Do you want the leadbreak upfront or in the middle?'

'In the middle. But keep the pace up. You've got to work that song hard, otherwise it's dead in the arse'.

'YER-RON!' George yells from the wings. We grab instruments, check hair and walk on, while George announces, 'Okay settle down, settle down. The Unknown Blues haven't arrived yet. Our opening act is a 4-piece unit called The Blitz. Expect great things from them in the future...' and omigod, he's making eyes at Samantha, who's come back inside and positioned herself in the front row, right in front of Mark.

'It's *You Really Got Me,'* says Jay. 'Are you ready Tom?'

'Ready as I'll ever be...!'

And just before we start, Mark pulls me aside and whispers, 'You do all the singing Tom, doan worry about Samantha...'

'Mate, I'm not the one who needs to worry about Samantha...' I indicate that she's chattin up George.

'Okay, let's kill em!' yells Jay hitting the power chords.

You Really Got Me, The Loved One, For Your Love, Do Wah Diddy Diddy and good applause. I love being onstage with these guys, I just hate the rehearsals.

Then omigod, Mark's losing the bass line in *My Generation.* I see the problem. Samantha and George are pashing. Mark is seething. Suddenly, I get a spark of an idea, pick up the acoustic guitar and stick on the false nose.

'Sort it!' I tell Mark. 'The next song,' I announce, '...is a daggy Aussie song called *Little Boy Lost...'.*

'Huh?' asks Jay, as Mark heads straight off stage, pushes through the crowd, has words with Samantha and starts shoving George.

'Mark's got a problem...' I reply to Jay, oom-chicka oom-chicka on guitar. 'Take a break mate...'. *In the wild Noo England ranges...*

I do it like we did it in Redfern. Hah! Some people laugh, but not too many cos most of them are watching the fight. Mark throws a punch, George ducks. Then George takes a swing, the bouncer grabs him, Mark climbs back onstage. The bouncer chucks George out. I can hear im shouting, 'But I'm in the next band!'

'Mark doesn't OWN me!' we hear Samantha yelling after George. Mark picks up his geetar and starts *Blues in E* cos he doesn't seem to know what he's doing. Jay calls out, *Communist Girls,* which we play. Then, *This Is It!* And off. ENCORE? But there's never an encore for an opening act.

I tell Salli, 'Wow, you heard that. Maybe splitting up is the wrong thing to do?'

'Snap out of it,' she says, 'You're a high skool band. You've gone about as far as you can.'

'What did you make of *Little Boy Lost?'*

'Funny.'

'I got away with it then?'

'Oh sure!' laughs Louise, joining in. 'It was wonderful, that stupid nose!' she chuckles, 'Oh, every song that comes on, Salli starts rockin and I start to rock too. She keeps telling me *stay cool/shut up.* Ha ha ha. Salli's great! Hey, I really embarrassed her at the Pymble Pub. I called out *Bloody Rockers!* to these guys in the corner bar. And when I looked around, I was the only one in the main bar, so they knew who said it. I was worried about Clayton though, they might go him if I didn't shut my mouth. Ha ha ha.' Bob's pretty pleased with the impression she's making.

'You were terrible!' Samantha tells me.

'And you were a fucken tart!'

'That's it!' snaps Samantha, 'I'm off then!'

'What's with her?'

'Not centre of attention,' says Mark.

The Mob are onstage now. George manages to get back inside with a caution. Doesn't matter. Him & Mark aren't mad at each other any more.

'Walked outta the pub and I had two ole women running after me for pinching flowers outta their front garden…!' Louise laughs on, '*Gerroff my garden*! Ha ha ha!'

'Well it's real nice meeting you Louise,' I say, kinda formally, 'you're terrific!'

'Well, it's GRATE seeing you guys on stage, especially Bob. He's so cute. He looks so groovy with his Hendrix hair and Byrds glasses. Where are those glasses?'

'Gone with Samantha,' he replies.

The Mob take a break. George comes over to our corner and offers Mark a smoke. Clayton pulls out his harp and starts playing something.

'Hey man, you're certainly improved!'

'Yup,' Clayton replies, 'I've bin practicing'.

'What's the book?' George points.

'The Bible,' sez Clayton, pulling it out of his coat.

'Huh?'

'Yup, Jesus was the first Hippie…'

'Huh?'

'He preached love & peace, had long hair and hitch-hiked around Jerusalem.'

'I was hitching outside Brisbane once…' says Jay, '…heading towards Toowoomba. (This is before I bought the bike.) And an 8-ton tipper truck pulled over, and this really big guy with a fat gut, blue singlet and stubbies sort-of, let me in. We were rollin along towards Darling Downs and he said, *Have you bin getting a bit lately?* I didn't have a girlfriend or anything at the time, so I just said to this repulsive bloke, *I've got a lady in Toowoomba* - ya know – *I'm doin fine.* Something to say, yeah. Next thing he's got his ole fella out and I was really freaked. I had a duffle bag with me and we were sort outside the border of Ipswich and there was a traffic light he had to stop at. I just bailed.'

'Yuk!'

'About six months later on that same stretch of road, I got picked up by someone who reminds me a lot of Stu. Pissed as. Driving flat-stick, never stopping for food or nuthin. He just gunned it all the way to Brissy…'. And then, turning back to Clayton, '…you were saying about hitch-hiking?'

'Maybe we hitch to Melbourne, instead of catching the Southern Flyer?'

'Anyone heard from Stu?'

'Yeah,' says Mark, 'he's working in a supermarket and bored out of his skull livin with his olds'.

'Why don't we move there?' I suggest.

'Sounds great,' says Jay, 'bout time I hit the road again'.

'Yeah…' says Mark, 'after the zams. But I thought you hated Stu?'

'Well, I didn't exackly *hate* im.'

'You didn't really get along wiv im that good,' Jay continues, 'You need to get down and drink wiv im to really appreciate Stu. Stu is the only guy I know who drove better pissed that he did straight. Full throttle when he hit the highway. Vmmm. Veecious.'

'He drove *drunk?'* asks Clayton, disturbed.

'Usually.'

The bands change over once more. This time it's Phil Jones & the Unknown Blues playing an excellent set. Clayton's dancing with someone we've never seen before. Louise is dancing with Bob, while we hang in our corner talking to Jay who's hanging onto the bottle. Me, Salli, and Mark have a swig now and then, but mostly it's Jay drinking and telling Stu-stories.

'I went with im to Bathurst at the beginning of the year. We went into a pub there and these four bikies walked in. Someone said something, I ferget what it woz but anyway, one of em hit me on the back of the neck and sent me flying. I was totally rubber from the beers anyway. I did the big gravel dive, got up, looked im over and thought, *He's too big and I'm too pissed.* So I turned to Stu and said, *Let's go.* So we walked out, got into the car. Next thing all these other guys came over from across the road, so there's just me and Stu and this army of bikers. Stu does this u-ey and they start kickin the car. He said to me, *They're damaging the paint! Get the gun! Get the gun!* Next, he told me to shoot this bloke. I was totally blind and outta my mind. As soon as he handed me the 22 I started yellin, *I can't hit im! Drive back! Drive back!* They all bolted back into the pub. And that's what I like about Stu - something always HAPPENS when you're wiv im. So count me in fer Melbourne!'

'How bout a dance before we split?' I ask Salli.

Mark starts worrying now, a bit, about Samantha, and then it's Equipment Time. Time to pack our gear and go. That empty after-the-dance feeling. Carrying heavy stuff. Helping the Unknown Blues with theirs. Meeting Phil Jones and not knowing what to say. Saying goodbye to everyone. Thanks for the gig.

Me & Salli are getting a lift with Clayton.

'How you getting home Mark?'

'Pillion with Jay.'

'How bout you two - Bob & Louise?'

'Louise's ole man's picking us up,' sez Bob.

'You know I'm preggers?' says Louise to Jay, as if he mightn't have already heard.

'Yup, by the time you're 30 you'll have a teenager! Yay! Here's to us!' Jay raises the bottle and has a final swig.

28
Subterranean Homesick Blues

Knock knock.

I'm through with dreaming.
I'm through with the Blitz.
I'm through with trying to tell people ideas they don't believe will work.
I'm through with skoolwork.
I'm through with being pushed around.
I'm through with ticket barriers, running the 440, writing lines, hair restrictions, 6th Form parties, young teachers, having to catch cricket balls, Science classes and standing in line.

Knock knock.

I want to paint.
I want to be a Kennedy. A *Morriss* Kennedy.
I want to be a bird. A Yardbird.
I want to be Dylan. Thomas.
Woody Guthrie's dead. He died of Huntington's Chorea and never quit smoking.
Bob Dylan isn't dead, but had a terrible motorbike accident that nearly buried him.
Maybe the Stones'll break up soon because everybody's been saying *Mick hates Brian* and *Brian hates Mick.*
The Beatles won't ever play live again. They can't hear a thing through the screams. They reckon they might as well mime.
I want to be a Jimi or a Jimmy. Hendrix or Page is okay.
I want to write *Howl* by Allen Ginsberg.
I want to write *It's All Right Ma, I'm Only Bleedin* by Bob Dylan.
I want to write *This Is It* by Bob.
I think I'm a bit pissed off that Bob's through with music. I don't think a wife and kid should come between mates.

Knock knock.

There's someone at the door.

I feel 1967 is a good year.
Sure it had its disappointments, but it checked out on points. We won. Everyone was good for me.
Shane, thanks.
Mum, thanks & sorry.
Dad, thanks for the Gibson Firebird.
Salli, you're the best.
Janet, you're the truest.

Pye, we'll see each other again.
Bob, it's not too late to come back, man.
Jay, I'll see you & Stu in Melbourne.
Mark, I'll see you there too…
The Boss – you'll get yours.
And Devlin, I'll see you in Hell.

Knock knock.

I open the door. It's Mark and a policeman.

'It's bin a bad night Tom,' says Mark, in grief.

Sorry about the pyjama top. Come in.

Do you want coffee?

Don't wake my parents?

What's a cop doing here?

Do you know what time it is?

How can it be a bad night? Last time we saw each other, it was fine.

'It's been a very bad night…' he sits down and adds, '…Jay's dead'.

Dead?

Hope I died before I get old.

Also, I don't believe him.

How can Jay be dead?

I feel light-headed. I get a bucket from the laundry and sit down.

Mum's hears this. I hear her getting out of bed. 'What's the matter?' she asks, 'What's this about?'

'Bike accident,' says the cop. He looks embarrassed. I want to vomit.

'Accident?' asks Mum, hauling her dressing gown.

She's never seen me cry before. Never seen the grown man cry. She saw me burst into tears when I ran my tricycle off the garden path and grazed my knee. She saw me howl when I broke my arm. She saw me sob when the gear slipped and I came off my pushbike. But she's never seen the grown man cry.

The cop explains some details, now it's Mum's turn to cry.

'The accident happened on the Pacific Highway between 12.30 and 1.00am this morning. I need to use your phone.' To the cop, it's just another teenage death, which is never just another teenage death.

In another couple of hours he might be doing exactly the same as this at someone else's place. Tonight I'm so sorry we call them *pigs.*

‘We were fair hiking along, then ran off the road,’ says Mark, holding his eye. ‘I tried to save him, but there was no chance.’

‘He *can’t* be dead! He was alive an hour ago! How can Jay be dead?’

Knock knock

There’s a policeman at the door with Mark & Jay.

Tom’s dead, they tell me. We’ve come to pick up the body.

‘I died in Vietnam,’ I reply. ‘I died in high school. I died of love.

I died of friendship. I died of Huntington’s Chorea. I can’t even remember my

own songs. Bury me please, with the Gibson.

‘I tried to save him, but couldn’t…’.

Mum snatches the phone from the cop. ‘You’re not telling this to his mother over the phone!’

‘No…’ he demures, ‘…I’m just phoning for her address’.

‘I really tried,’ Mark continues, Mark who never ever cries, ‘I was thrown clear, I came off the back. Jay somersaulted forwards and I heard this crack when he hit the pole. I raced over. There was all this gunk coming outta his mouth…’

‘But couldn’t you have *tried?’*

Knock knock.

The Grim Reaper is at the door.

Behind him – Woody Guthrie, Magritte, Brian Epstein and all the

1967 Dead.

‘What year is it now?’ I ask.

‘Sooner than you think.’

‘The minute I saw him, I knew - I knew straight away.’

‘Couldn’t you have tried *harder?’*

‘I tried punching his heart, put a coat over him and ran to the nearest house. A car pulled up before I reached the gate. They called the ambos. I went back. But it wasn’t *him* any more. He looked all right, except for this stuff coming out of his mouth…’. He gets a look of horror as he says, ‘…I even tried mouth-to-mouth’.

‘What’s going on?’ says Dad, ‘What’s the problem’.

‘It’s Jay,’ says Mum, ‘he’s dead’.

Then a weird thing happens. Dad puts his arm around me, hugs me and asks if I’m all right.

'I ran to the nearest house!' Mark continues, the cop silently standing beside him. Then Mark stops and says, 'What's wrong with my eye?'

Mum throws her arms around Mark. 'You poor kid,' she weeps, 'you poor poor kids!'

29

Paper Sun

How can someone be dead only one hour after you've seen him walk and talk and laugh and drink and dance?

As everyone files out of the room, Jay's spirit enters.

'Can you hear me Jay?'

I can hear you Tom. Push a little harder and I'll take on a shape.
I can be a spirit if you want. And I'll play you another song, tell you another hitchhiking yarn and borrow your Gibson.
I always had my eye on your new guitar.

I'll show you the future – your mother's gravestone over here. The year of her death reads 2002. I'll show you where your father is buried.
As for Cousin Ken, well – he might as well have died in Vietnam.
And see that headstone – the one over here, with the words 'Hope I die before I get old'? That one's yours mate.
There's even the year of your death. You could give up now mate.
It won't make any difference, except to your kids.

'Kids?'

Yes Tom, children.
Everyone has children except me.
Push a little harder and you can call me up.
I could materialize right now if you command the spirits to release me. Push Tom, push.

And we could play one last song, I could be right by your side.

But it wouldn't be me, because I'm dead.

'Jay! Jay! Don't go! Tell me – one last thing, now you're up there with Woody. Tell me – will I live until I'm 30?'

No Tom, you'll never reach 30.

You & me will be 18 forever.

30

1968

Linda Lee
LRT-1967 A 45RPM
TIME:3.30
COPYRIGHT CONTROL
COMMUNIST GIRLS
(Tom Truscott, Bob Sims) (Aust. Comp.)
THE BLITZ

Also by Lowell Tarling

Fiction

Taylor's Troubles – first edition 1982
Taylor's Troubles – revised edition 2004
The Secret Gang of Oomlau – 1988
1967, This Is It! – 1990

Anthologies

Hunter Valley Poets 1973-1973
All The Best, A Selection Celebrating 25 Years of Puffins in Australia – 1989
Australia's Best Poetry Volume One – 2001
Visions From The Valley, Poetry of the Hunter Valley 1960-2000 – 2001
The Great Australian Shed - 2012

Non-Fiction

Thank God for the Salvos, The Salvation Army In Australia 1880-1980 – 1980
The Edges of Seventh-day Adventism – 1981
The Australian Handbook of Business Letters – 1989
17 Small Business Success Stories – 1991
Gold Beyond Your Dreams (with Heather Turland) – 1998
No More Cellulite Fast (with Violetta Chevell) – 1999
Beyond Azaria (with Michael Chamberlain) – 1999
Brash Business (with Geoff Brash) – 2000
The Complete Tiny Tim Interviews – 2000
Breadwinner (with Tom O'Toole) – 2000
The Women's Club (with Di Williams) – 2000
My Dad Thinks I Rob Banks (with Joe Sammon) – 2001
Risky Business (with Clare Loewenthal) – 2001
Secrets of the Beechworth Bakery (with Tom O'Toole) – 2001
Guilty to Driza-Bone (with Frank Fisher) – 2002
The Method, A Writer's Handbook-2003
The Business Method, the A-Z of Business Communications – 2004
On The End of a Wire (with Peter Davidson) – 2004
Go For Your Life! (with Chris Grey) – 2005
Busted: 17 Classic Mythbusters – 2007
South Side Story – 2008
Coping with Difficult People – 2010
Coping with Parents – 2010
Coping with Teenagers – 2011
Coping with So!! Difficult People – Three books in one – 2012
Tiny Tim – Tiptoe Through A Lifetime – 2013
Song-Poems & Rhymes – 2013

www.lowelltarling.com.au
lowell@lowelltarling.com.au

Printed in Australia
AUHW011336220720
331157AU00001B/1

9 781922 384126